THE DREYFUS AFFAIR

THE DREYFUS AFFAIR

A NATIONAL SCANDAL

BETTY SCHECHTER

Illustrated with photographs

1965

HOUGHTON MIFFLIN COMPANY BOSTON

Also by Betty Schechter

THE PEACEABLE REVOLUTION

CONTENTS

To my parents

" . . . a single injustice, a single illegality, especially if it be officially confirmed, a single insult offered to justice and to right, especially if it be generally, nationally, conveniently accepted, is enough to dishonor and disgrace an entire nation."

Charles Péguy

"I AM INNOCENT"

I

Who Is the Scoundrel D. ?

THE CHAPEL of St. Clotilde was almost empty. It was eight o'clock on a September evening in 1894 and as the day lingered high in the sky above Paris, dusk gathered on the streets below. Most Parisians were at their dinners. Inside the church flickering candlelight revealed only two women and a child — a mother and her daughter on their knees in a pew toward the rear of the church, and in a forward pew an older woman kneeling, head bowed over her folded hands.

The mother stood up, took her child by the hand and quietly left the church. Several moments later, the other woman raised her head and looked around. Seeing all the other pews empty, she laboriously rose to her feet, picked up a paper bag from the floor where she had been kneeling, and walked toward the door. In the shadows at the rear of the church a huge man leaned against a pillar, waiting. Approaching him, the woman paused. She glanced around once more and, seeing no one, she handed the man the paper bag. He, in turn, gave her an envelope. No words passed between them. The woman put the envelope in her pocket and then quickly walked out of the church. The man remained behind. A few minutes later he, too, left. Coat collar turned up, his bowler hat slanted down over his eyes, the paper bag tucked under his arm, he strode off, his footsteps echoing through the quiet streets.

The man was Major Hubert Henry of the Statistical Section of the French General Staff. The woman was Madame Marie Bastian, a middle-aged cleaning woman who spent her days washing windows, scrubbing floors and tidying offices at the German Embassy on the Rue de Lille. The paper bag she handed to the major contained gleanings — crumpled letters and memoranda and scraps of paper with writing on them — from the German Embassy's wastebaskets. The major and the cleaning woman met in this fashion regularly, twice a month.

Madame Bastian grumbled to herself as she made her way home after leaving Major Henry; she thought that she worked hard enough during the day and was entitled to her rest when evening came. The major, however, insisted on staging all their rendezvous after dark and Madame Bastian complied for love of the money in the envelopes he gave her.

Arriving at his home on the Rue Duquesne, Major Henry announced to his wife that he wanted his dinner at once as there were certain papers that demanded his urgent attention. Madame Henry did not mention that dinner had been ready and waiting for some time, nor did she question her husband about what had kept him so late or about the nature of the papers he was so anxious to get to. She knew that he was engaged in highly secret work for the Army, work that required him to meet with strange people, in odd places and at inconvenient hours and she was used to keeping the dinner warm until whatever hour he appeared. She hoped, however, that whatever her husband's urgent business was, it could be satisfactorily dealt with that very night for his leave was due to start the next day. Madame Henry had been looking forward to a vacation for a long time and she was sure that she would lose her sweetly reasonable attitude toward her husband's work if, at the last minute, it interfered with their leaving Paris as planned.

As soon as he had had his coffee, the major retired to his study with Madame Bastian's paper bag. Spilling its contents out onto his desk, he set to work. With great care he smoothed out crumpled papers, matched up torn scraps with other scraps, attached these together with gummed tape and pasted them on backing sheets. Then, lighting a cigarette, he began to study each of the jigsaw puzzles he had completed. Was there anything he could use? An hour later Henry stubbed out his third cigarette and sighed. No, unfortunately, there was nothing this time. His whole evening's work had been for nothing; the memoranda, letters and notes he had so carefully reconstructed all dealt with trivialities; they were exactly the sort of thing for which the wastepaper basket had been invented. Too bad. In the past, Henry had found many treasures in Madame Bastian's paper bags and he was badly disappointed at not having found any in this one. If there had been even one he would have given up his leave. The business of the Statistical Section was counterespionage and Madame Bastian, in her position of trusted employee at the German Embassy, was one of the Section's most valuable sources of information.

Counterespionage presupposes espionage. Was there espionage emanating from the German Embassy? On more than one occasion the German Ambassador, Count Georg Munster, had publicly stated there was not. Count Munster, an elderly, able, career diplomat, believed such spying activity on the part of his staff to be detrimental to the successful performance of his own diplomatic duties and he was so opposed to it that when, several years earlier, he had discovered that the officer who was serving then as his military attaché was spying for the German General Staff behind his back, he had seen to it that the man was promptly recalled to Berlin. Munster made a public announcement at that time to the effect that spying was absolutely forbidden to everyone at the German Embassy. Nevertheless, thanks to Madame Bastian, the French Statistical Section had excellent reason to believe that the new German military attaché, Colonel Max von Schwartzkoppen, was following the example of his predecessor and, taking his orders directly from the German generals in Berlin, was masterminding an extensive network of spies in France.

What was it that the German generals were so anxious to find out? Generally, they were interested in all matters pertaining to French military strength; specifically, they were extremely curious about the military implications of the recently concluded alliance between France and Russia.

France and Germany had been at peace since 1870 when Germany had inflicted a crushing defeat on France at Sedan in the concluding battle of the Franco-Prussian war. Stripping the vanquished nation of her border provinces of Alsace and Lorraine and saddling her with an enormous war debt, the Germans had thought that they were completely canceling France out as a threat to them for at least fifty years and for a time Frenchmen thought the same thing. Indeed, during the first months after the war, the people of France lived in constant fear of a surprise German attack along the new, still unfortified border. But, before very long, the fear in their hearts made room for a spirit of determination and a dark, angry hope. Within three years after the war, France paid off the German war debt that was supposed to cripple her for a generation; national pride was reborn and there came into being a national obsession. Frenchmen of every

class — aristocracy, bourgeoisie, peasantry — all Frenchmen
were gripped by an overpowering desire for revenge.

Revenge! How sweetly the word rang in French ears! It
was a magic word conjuring up visions of a France whole
again, a France risen once more to the glory that had been
hers under the Kings, a nation restored to her historical
grandeur. Vengeance on the hated German conquerors! So
seductive was the idea that by the 1880's there was no longer
any doubt in the minds of the French people — France
must have her revenge. And how was she to achieve it?
With her Army, of course — the great Army of the Revolution, the triumphant Army of Napoleon. Alas, it was true
that the English had defeated Napoleon at Waterloo and
that the Second Empire of Napoleon III had toppled before
the Germans at Sedan, but most Frenchmen were sure that
betrayal, not military weakness, had brought France to her
knees at Sedan and they were certain that with hard work and
sacrifice and, above all, with faith in her Army, France could
rise again to power. In 1893 Frenchmen heard thrilling
rumors, supposedly originating with "those in the know," of
a vast Army master plan for a counterattack against Germany. When, in 1894, news of the ratification of a military
pact with Russia was released, the whole nation rejoiced;
with this pact France had clearly taken a giant step toward
her national goal of revenge.

The German General Staff, well aware that the French-
Russian alliance boded ill for the German-weighted balance
of power in Europe, ordered their military attaché in Paris,
Colonel von Schwartzkoppen, to find out by whatever means
he could, just what the new pact meant in terms of revised
French mobilization plans, new fortifications systems and
new weaponry. In carrying out these orders he took pains

to cover his tracks well; he had to hide his espionage activities from not only the French but from his own Ambassador as well. As far as Munster was concerned he succeeded; the Ambassador thought his attaché was occupied exclusively with his routine duties of arranging border patrols and issuing visas to French citizens who wished to visit relatives in German-held Alsace and Lorraine.

Munster was fooled but the French Statistical Section was not. They not only knew what von Schwartzkoppen was after but they also knew that he was having a small but disturbing measure of success. Several French military maps of border areas had mysteriously disappeared and the Statistical Section learned that they had found a home in the German Embassy when Major Henry pasted together a draft of a note addressed to the Italian military attaché, Colonel Panizzardi, and written in what Henry recognized as von Schwartzkoppen's hand, which read:

> Enclosed are twelve detail maps of Nice that the Scoundrel D. left with me for you. I told him that you had no intention of taking up relations with him again. He said that there was a misunderstanding and that he will do his best to satisfy you . . .

Who was the "Scoundrel D." and how had he come into possession of French military maps? Was it possible that he was actually in the French Army? By the end of 1893 the Section had good reason to believe that it was. Late in December of that year Colonel Henry pieced together a draft of another von Schwartzkoppen memorandum from fragments of paper brought to him by Madame Bastian and although this one lacked several pieces it was complete enough to chill the blood of the French officers who read it:

> Doubt . . . proof . . . Officer . . . Dangerous situation
> for me with a French officer . . . not to negotiate per-
> sonally . . .

Three months later the picture darkened even more; a part-
time spy, formerly employed by the Section, hinted to a
French intelligence agent that "there is a traitor in your
midst."

As the pieces of evidence pointing to the existence of a
French traitor piled up, a current of apprehension ran
through the Statistical Section and, from it, through the
upper echelons of the French General Staff. A security check
was immediately placed on all the agents employed by the
Statistical Section and the French Intelligence Service.
There was always the possibility that one of them had
succumbed to the temptation of serving, and being paid by,
two masters. French spies of unquestionable loyalty to their
country were assigned to spy on other French spies of
equally unassailable loyalty. In an attempt to mislead von
Schwartzkoppen, the Section manufactured "official" documents containing false information and these, together with
a few genuine papers of negligible value, were given to
French agents instructed to pose as traitors and to sell the
"package" to von Schwartzkoppen. So frenzied were these
efforts to put the Germans on a false scent that it was said in
the halls of the War Ministry that not even the top men in
the Statistical Section could keep track of which papers the
agents carried in their breast pockets were genuine and
which contrived. In spite of all these countermeasures, the
Section learned via the contents of Madame Bastian's paper
bags that the trickle of bona fide information to von
Schwartzkoppen was unchecked.

From the very top, from the Minister of War himself,

General Auguste Mercier, the word came down to the Section: Find the traitor with all possible speed! Conduct the search under a heavy cloak of secrecy! Although it was entirely natural that General Mercier, as Minister of War, should be anxious to stop up a leak of information to the Germans, compelling personal reasons, more than official zeal, dictated his emphasis on haste and secrecy. Recently several matters handled by the Ministry of War had turned out badly and Mercier had been sharply criticized for "bumbling inefficiency" by powerful groups in Parliament that opposed a republican form of government for France and by the anti-Republic newspapers that spoke for them. Mercier knew that he could expect these same elements to pounce on the slightest excuse to further discredit him and, through him, the Premier, the rest of the Cabinet and the Republic itself. General Mercier had no special love for the Republic but he did hold both his reputation and his well-paying job as Minister of War in high esteem. If the traitor was unmasked speedily he would lose neither. If, on the other hand, news of the traitor's existence leaked out while he was still at large, a "stupid and incompetent" Minister of War would almost certainly be turned out of office.

Why was there so much anti-Republic sentiment in Parliament and in the press? The truth was that, since its birth in 1871, the Third Republic had never been secure in the affections of the French people and by the 1880's a great many Frenchmen had come to seriously distrust their democratic form of government. There were widespread complaints about the Republic's instability; a man couldn't even turn his back for a moment, it was said, without finding on facing forward again that another Premier and his Cabinet had fallen. Many Catholic Frenchmen, pointing to the fact

that France was and always had been a predominantly
Catholic country, maintained that the Republic's insistence
on political equality for all citizens left France dangerously
open to betrayal. These Catholics were sure that French
Protestants were secretly supporting the aims of Protestant
England and they said that since all Jews were by nature
prone to treachery it was only logical to assume that French
Jews were conspiring to sell France to her enemies. Many
French Protestants, on the other hand, while vigorously
affirming their own wholehearted devotion to their country,
shared the belief that French Jews were acting as agents for
enemy powers. A recent rash of financial scandals had made
bad matters worse; when official investigations of the scandals
revealed that a number of elected representatives of the
people had not been above selling their votes in Parliament
for personal gain, millions of Frenchmen concluded that
corruption was an inevitable by-product of democracy.

In the city of Paris, historically the center of French political activity, a great many people were convinced that the
answer to their country's future lay in her past. They argued
that what France needed most was a single, strong leader —
a "good king," perhaps, or a benevolent military dictator
— in any case, a man who would lean heavily on the political
wisdom of the Catholic Church. While Parisians waited for
such a man to appear and consolidate a following behind
him, provincial Frenchmen continued to vote Republican
Senators and Deputies to Parliament. Memories of pre-Revolution aristocratic tyranny were still strong among the
peasants of France and they knew that the Republic, with
all its faults, could at least be trusted to keep the heel of the
aristocracy off their necks.

Seriously divided as the people of France were on the

question of how their country should be governed, they were as one on the subject of the French Army. All Frenchmen loved their Army. Their protection against dreaded external enemies, it was at the same time the instrument for their ardently desired revenge against Germany. Too, its officer class was a reassuring link with France's glorious past, the days when the nation was ruled by a coalition of king, church and aristocracy. Although the Great Revolution had shorn the Church of its political power and the aristocracy of its political privileges, the prestige of both lived on in the army officer class, in the late 1800's, as in the old pre-Revolution days, almost all officers in the French Army were sons of the old nobility who had received their early education with the learned Jesuit priests. Even the peasants were content to allow the Army to remain a bastion of aristocratic strength. Their political liberties secure, they, like all Frenchmen, were proud to have their soldier-sons led by such well-born, highly educated and Church-influenced gentlemen.

Thus, General Mercier was in an ambiguous position. As a general of the Army he was loved and admired by the whole French people; as a not very efficient Minister of the Republic, however, he was constantly kept busy warding off scathing political attacks. Now, in the summer of 1894, he told the chief of the Statistical Section, Colonel Jean Sandherr, that it would be foolish to hope that the existence of a traitor in the French Army could be kept a department secret much longer. He said that there was certain to be an information leak soon and he told Sandherr that if the Section had not found the traitor before then they would surely all be out of their jobs.

Who was the "Scoundrel D."? Who was the officer who

had placed the German military attaché in "a dangerous position"? The Statistical Section hummed with activity as each member of its staff bent his every effort toward finding the answers to these nagging questions. A twenty-four hour watch was placed on the German Embassy and Madame Bastian's harvests were picked over with meticulous care, but the traitor's identity remained a tantalizing mystery. Colonel Sandherr grew more anxious with each passing day. Already ill with the disease that would kill him three years later, he had been finding it increasingly difficult to cope with his job of directing the French counterespionage effort and he had recently let a number of important matters slide; now, the added pressure from the Minister of War compounded his troubles. In desperation, he put Major Hubert Henry in personal charge of the Section's efforts to find the mysterious traitor.

Outwardly, Major Henry appeared to be the very model of a French Army officer. Unusually tall and heavily built, he carried both his height and his weight well; his long mustache was curled at the ends in the military style and he had the high color and clear complexion of a healthy child. When, head held high, he walked along the boulevards, splendid in his black, multi-buttoned, gold-braided tunic, black trousers and visored kepi, he seemed to exude robust strength and competence. He impressed the people he passed as exactly the sort of man that France would do well to place her trust in. But Major Henry was not treated by his fellow officers in the War Ministry with the respect that would seem to be his due. The reason lay in the circumstances of his birth. Major Henry was the son of peasants; the other officers were all wealthy men with distinguished titles sprinkled liberally on their family trees.

At a time when his associates were attending St. Cyr, the fashionable Jesuit-run military academy that would prepare them for their Army careers, Hubert Henry was laboriously pulling himself up through the noncommissioned ranks. The high-born St. Cyr cadets received their commissions upon graduation as a matter of course; Henry owed his to a combination of outstanding bravery on the battlefield and the lingering influence of Napoleon who had insisted on injecting the French Army with the democratic principles of the Great Revolution. Napoleon's democratizing vaccination had not taken well in the higher echelons where the aristocracy did its best to monopolize the officer class. Nevertheless, an occasional exceptionally courageous, ambitious and hardworking nonaristocrat could crash the officer ranks. This Henry had done and he had gone even further — by gaining a reputation for single-minded devotion to the Army and willingness to undertake all the least pleasant assignments, he had been able to push his way to a position on the General Staff. On the social level, however, his success story did not mitigate the facts of his low birth. Henry's fellow officers accepted him as a working associate but at the end of the day, they drew a social curtain which effectively shut him out of their world. The snubs cut and Henry's only consolation was his knowledge that there was one officer-aristocrat who occasionally sought his company. Several years earlier, Count Major Ferdinand Walsin-Esterhazy had been assigned to the Statistical Section on temporary duty as a translator and when he was reassigned away from the Section he had unaccountably made it a point to keep in touch with Henry.

Esterhazy and Henry did not meet often but in view of the rigidly stratified social system that prevailed in France in those days and considering the vast differences between the personalities of the two men, it was more than a little odd that they met at all. Henry, his peasant background obvious in his coarse accent and often vulgar choice of words, was stolid, serious, and entirely lacking in social graces. Esterhazy's family background, while a bit too international for the taste of some of his peers, was distinguished; he was of a flighty turn of mind, his behavior was completely unpredictable and his reputation was one of the worst in Paris. It was well known that he had run through his wife's considerable dowery in short order and had thereupon left Madame Esterhazy to shift entirely for herself while he found his amusement in the company of a succession of ladies, fashionable and unfashionable, married and unmarried. He was in constant financial difficulties and although he could be a charming and gay companion at times, he was usually so preoccupied with his acute need for money that he was enveloped in a cloud of gloom from which he issued dire threats to blackmail people in high places or to commit suicide if he was not granted the loans he was after at the moment.

The Henry-Esterhazy association was a strange one but Henry, dazzled by Esterhazy's title and impressed by the dashing figure the Count cut with his aristocratic bearing, polished manners, stylishly drooping mustache and romantic, dark, fiery eyes, did not think to wonder why Esterhazy occasionally asked him out to dine. Sitting in an expensive restaurant and listening to the Count's amusing tales of his amorous adventures, Henry enjoyed himself and felt flattered by the interest the high-born officer seemed to take in him. When Esterhazy confided in him his hopes for a permanent position on the General Staff and asked Henry to help him if he could, Henry's pride, bruised by the snobbery of the

General Staff officers, was pleasantly soothed. When Ester-hazy introduced Henry to some of his friends, Henry was predisposed to like them. One of these friends was Edouard Drumont, the famous author and editor of the anti-Semitic paper, *La Libre Parole*. Henry was impressed by Drumont's renown and by his solemn, scholarly aspect and, having always been suspicious of Jews himself, Henry found it easy to go along with Drumont's extreme brand of racist hatred.

In September of 1894, however, Henry was not thinking about Esterhazy or his friends. He had not seen the Count for some time and, besides, he was almost totally absorbed in his efforts to get ahead. He saw a shining avenue to further success opening up with the Army's frantic search for the traitor. Colonel Sandherr was seriously ill and it would not be long before the question of his successor as Chief of the Statistical Section would come up; if, by that time, Henry had tracked down and exposed von Schwartzkoppen's mysterious "contact," the question, Henry felt sure, would be easily answered. But he knew that if he was to succeed he would have to have further and more detailed evidence to work on. To know that a traitor existed and that he was referred to by von Schwartzkoppen as "the Scoundrel D." was not nearly enough. What was really wanted was a sample of the man's handwriting.

It was Henry's bad luck to be away on his leave when the "bordereau" was brought into the Statistical Section, for with that document, written in a small, neat, slightly slanting hand, the Statistical Section received its first solid clues to the identity of the traitor.

2

The Bordereau

A CERTAIN Martin Brücker, one of Colonel Sandherr's staff of part-time spies, had been hanging around the German Embassy on the Rue de Lille one day late in September of 1894. At intervals he had strolled past the door of the Embassy and glanced inside. Each time he had seen the Embassy's concierge on duty behind the desk in the lobby. Then, late in the afternoon, as he lounged in a nearby doorway, Brücker had seen the concierge come out of the Embassy accompanied by a man he knew to be her husband and, as the agent watched, the couple walked in the direction of a nearby bistro. Guessing that the concierge would be away from her post long enough to have a leisurely glass of wine, Brücker walked into the Embassy and, finding the lobby unattended, he went behind the desk and audaciously snatched a letter from a pigeonhole that appeared to be reserved for incoming mail. When he was safely home, Brücker opened the envelope and scanned its contents. He was elated by what he saw; it seemed to him that he had got onto something important, something for which the Statistical Section would pay him well. Of late, the officers of the Section had been complaining that the stuff he was bringing them was worthless. Brücker was sure that this letter would make them change their tune. He usually made his deliveries to Major Henry but, knowing that Henry was away on leave, he took the stolen paper straight to Colonel Sandherr.

Sandherr felt ill when he saw what Brücker had brought him. The unsigned letter, addressed to von Schwartzkoppen, was what the French call a "bordereau," a covering list, and its contents catalogued a variety of French military matters. Each item listed referred to specific information which the author of the letter clearly intended to deliver to von Schwartzkoppen under separate cover. Here, before Sandherr's eyes, was apparent proof that the traitor the Section had to deal with was more of a threat than had been supposed; the man seemed to be dangerously well informed. The bordereau mentioned results of tests on a new infantry weapon and the deployment of troops to enhance its power. Reference was also made to "a modification to the artillery formations" and the last item on the list concerned "the preliminary Firing Manual of the Field Artillery" which, the unknown author wrote, was "extremely difficult to come by" and would only be at his disposal for a very few days.

Seriously worried by what he read, Sandherr tried to console himself with the thought that now at last the Section had a sample of the traitor's handwriting. What a pity it was that Major Henry was on leave; this letter would be right up his alley! It was clear to Sandherr, however, that this portentous piece of paper could not wait on Henry's return. He called in the other officers attached to the Section and together they all puzzled over the riddle of the bordereau.

Who could have written it? Before long the conferring officers had agreed that only someone on the General Staff or someone closely connected with the General Staff could have knowledge of all the matters referred to in the document. The General Staff! Ah, matters were serious indeed. The bordereau was quickly circulated among the Minister of War, the Chief of Staff and the Chiefs and Deputy Chiefs of the four Bureaus of the General Staff in the hopes that one of them would recognize the handwriting. No one did, but one Deputy Chief deduced from the bordereau's contents that its author probably had an artillery background and might well have gained his knowledge of the non-artillery matters referred to while serving as a probationer, an officer assigned on temporary duty to each of the four Bureaus of the General Staff before being permanently assigned to one of them. A list of the probationers was taken from the files and examined. Anxious eyes scanned the list and stopped at one name, that of Captain Alfred Dreyfus. Dreyfus! That would clear up the puzzle of "the Scoundrel D."! The biographical information beside Dreyfus's name revealed that he was an artillery captain who, as a probationer, had passed through all four Bureaus. And, to top it all off, Dreyfus was a Jew — the only Jew on the General Staff.*

Sandherr clapped his hand to his forehead and exclaimed, "Why didn't I think of it?" Sandherr was well known as a bitter anti-Semite and now he reminded the other officers that he had tried without success to block Dreyfus's appointment to the General Staff. The colonel asked each officer his opinion of Dreyfus and though no one of them could say he knew the man well, each expressed an unfavorable general impression of him. Dreyfus, it seemed, was pompous, overly self-sufficient, too withdrawn; he was a prig; he was entirely too anxious to get ahead and too curious about military matters that were not properly his concern.

Letters Dreyfus had written were taken from the files and compared with the bordereau. Were the handwritings the

---

* In France, Dreyfus is pronounced DRAY-*FOOS*; in the United States, it is usually pronounced *DRY*-FUS but *DRAY*-FUS is also acceptable.

same? No, unfortunately they were not. There were, however, definite similarities between them. One officer pointed out that Dreyfus might well have tried to disguise his hand while writing the bordereau and that if he had, it would account for the disparities between the hands. On his suggestion identifying marks on Dreyfus's letters were masked out and a handwriting expert from Banque de France was called in and asked to compare the letters with the bordereau. His opinion was disappointing. It was entirely possible, he said, that one man had written the bordereau and another the letters.

Alphonse Bertillon, a noted Police Department statistician, was consulted next. Bertillon did not exactly qualify as a handwriting expert — he had won his fame by devising a method of identifying criminals by a mathematical analysis of the bone structure of their skulls — but on being asked by one of his friends in the Statistical Section if he would apply his mathematical expertise to a problem of handwriting analysis he was happy to oblige. A little man with wiry black hair and a bushy black beard, Bertillon set to his task armed with an impressive array of magnifying glasses and measuring devices. He had no idea of who was thought to be the author of the exhibits he was examining but his officer friend had let it drop that the War Office believed them all to have been written by one man. He bustled about between the bordereau and the letters, held each up to the light, measured individual characters and covered page after page of scratch paper with complicated calculations. At last he gave his opinion: there could be no doubt, he announced, that one man had written each of the samples. He immediately launched into an explanation of the system he had used in arriving at his conclusion but, when it turned out that he had relied on multiple sets of figures that balanced, counter-balanced, and apparently contradicted each other, the Section's officers gave up trying to follow him and patiently waited for him to finish. His system was incomprehensible but his conclusion was the one they had all been hoping for and it was gratefully accepted.

General Mercier was overjoyed when he heard of Bertillon's opinion. The sinister implications of the bordereau had unnerved him and he had angrily pressed Colonel Sandherr to redouble his efforts to unmask the traitor. Even when Sandherr had assured him that the Section had a promising suspect in Captain Dreyfus he had been only slightly mollified. Fire flashing from his hooded eyes, the slim, sallow general had paced the floor of his office demanding that Sandherr produce evidence that Dreyfus actually was the man they were after. Now Bertillon's opinion seemed to him to be that evidence and he wanted to take action at once. Dreyfus accused, arrested, tried and convicted with dispatch would be an impressive demonstration of the administrative efficiency of an aroused War Minister who had found to his horror that a traitor walked among his officers. True, the cold light of publicity would reveal the awful fact that an agent for the Germans had been allowed to penetrate the hallowed sanctum of the General Staff; still, if that agent turned out to be a Jew, the shame could be borne. After all, Mercier told his aides, the fact that Jews were allowed to occupy high Army positions was a national misfortune that could not be blamed on him.

Cooler heads cautioned Mercier against precipitate action; it would be better to wait, they said, until further evidence of Dreyfus's treachery could be found. They pointed out that if Dreyfus were tried on the basis of the bordereau, it would be difficult to keep the Germans from learning that a document had been stolen from their Embassy and the whole matter might well explode into an international incident of awesome proportions. Others, close enough to Mercier to be frank, warned him that as far as he, personally, was concerned, all would surely be lost if it turned out that he had acted too hastily — if the evidence against Dreyfus proved in court to be insufficient. But General Mercier was in a hurry. He assured his aides that once Dreyfus was in custody his effects could be searched and more evidence would be found and, because Mercier occupied the top rung of a ladder they all dreamed of climbing, his subordinates found themselves able to accommodate their ways of thinking to his. Mercier issued orders for Dreyfus to be called on the carpet and arrested. The general's apprehensive subordinates consoled themselves with the thought that, once accused, Dreyfus might confess — he might even save himself and everybody else a great deal of trouble by committing suicide. After all, they told each other, the fact that Dreyfus was a Jew made it highly likely that he was the traitor they were seeking. Of all the officers thus far involved in the search for the traitor, only Sandherr was an avowed anti-Semite, but in the makeup of each of them there was what was considered in France in those days to be "the normal amount of anti-Semitism."

Why was it that in the 1890's in France, in an enlightened age and in a country that had lighted the path to democracy for the rest of Europe, a certain amount of anti-Semitism was considered "normal"? It was because times had been hard in France ever since the crushing defeat at Sedan and, as the years had passed, more and more Frenchmen had found it convenient to lay their country's difficulties on the doorstep of the Jews. Unemployment plagued the cities and it was said that Jewish manipulation of the money markets was causing economic disruptions, drying up jobs and draining the nation's wealth into foreign bank accounts. Many attributed the rise of the worker class with its insistent demands and its frightening outbursts of terrorist activity to the Jews. The nation fell victim to a virulent "conspiracy fever"; almost everyone was convinced that a weak and corrupt French government was at the mercy of those who were plotting to betray France and sell her to her enemies. There was some disagreement on the identity of the plotters. Some said it was the Protestants, others, the Freemasons or the Jesuit and Assumptionist religious orders; most Frenchmen, however, thought it was the Jews.

Ancient superstitions and myths were revived and Jews were spoken of as "strangers" and "rootless wanderers," a people whose inter-European family ties led to divided loyalties. In 1886 a book, *La France Juive,* stating that the Jews were at the root of all French woes, was published and widely read. Its author, Edouard Drumont, proposed that this "infidel people" should be expelled from the country and their property confiscated. The sensation the book caused was short-lived; its author's recommendations for a solution to the "Jewish problem" were so radical and flamboyant that few Frenchmen could take them seriously. Six years later, Drumont launched a newspaper, *La Libre Parole,* with a series of articles denouncing all Jewish Army officers as potential traitors. Again the extremist's ferocious anti-Semitism found little favor among the general populace and when, as a result of a rash of duels sparked by the offensive articles, a Jewish army captain was killed, Drumont was criticized on all sides. A few months later, however, in the autumn of 1892, the Panama Canal Affair burst wide open and Drumont's star rose again.

The scheme to cut a canal through the Panama Isthmus had been poorly planned from the start and its master mind, Ferdinand de Lesseps, the engineer-hero of the Suez Canal, had disastrously underestimated its cost. Short of funds almost as soon as the job was underway, de Lesseps hired two Jews as "middlemen" to buy silence from a critical press and to bribe members of the French Parliament into backing a public loan to finance his Panama Canal Company. The company failed and the whole affair ended as a financial fiasco. Thousands of middle-class Frenchmen lost their hard-earned savings in a venture that high government officials had assured them was risk-free. Everyone involved in the scandal had been corrupt — de Lesseps, the two Jewish middlemen he had hired, and the Deputies and Senators they had bribed — but public anger and resentment found its target in the Jews. Each day, *La Libre Parole* printed new exposés and revelations about "wicked Jewish financiers" and the newspaper's circulation soared. The Jews, said Drumont over and over again, only the Jews had brought thousands of Frenchmen to financial ruin.

3

Captain Alfred Dreyfus

DRUMONT's rabid anti-Semitism found fertile soil at the Ecole de Guerre, the postgraduate military school that prepared promising young officers for the General Staff. Raised within a narrow, highly conservative framework that stressed the overweening values of family, Church and country, the high-born officer students and instructors at the Ecole were ripe for suspicion of the "alien" Jews against whom Drumont railed and the Republic he attacked indirectly through the Jews. All but a very few of the students had come to the Ecole with the "proper" background for an army officer — wealth, aristocratic lineage and Jesuit-led early schooling — and they looked on those of their fellow students who lacked this background as inferiors. Jews were regarded as especially presumptuous "outsiders." In 1892, when *La Libre Parole*'s attack on Jewish army officers appeared, Alfred Dreyfus, a thirty-three-year-old artillery captain, was one of only two Jews at the Ecole and he found the going rough indeed. One of his instructors publicly stated that he did not like to see Jews go to the General Staff and another so obviously downgraded one of Dreyfus's examinations that the young captain applied for relief to the director of the school who, though he admitted to Dreyfus that the mark was unfair, did nothing to change it. Running an uphill race with brilliant young noblemen who had everything working for them, Dreyfus stuck close to his books, determined to make up for the handicap his Jewishness placed on him by hard work and outstanding performance.

As a boy of eleven, Dreyfus had seen his beloved home province of Alsace wrested from France by the hated Germans and as a young man he had vowed that he would someday play a part in avenging Alsace. Resisting his older brothers' pleas to join them in the family's thriving textile business, he had embarked on a military career when he was nineteen. On the strength of his excellent school record he was admitted to the military college, the Ecole Polytechnique, and after his graduation he went first to the artillery school at Fontainebleau and then to the School of Explosives at Bourges. It was at Bourges that he met Lucie Hadamard, the daughter of a wealthy Paris diamond merchant. In 1890 he and Lucie were married and on his wedding day Dreyfus received word that he had won a highly coveted place in the Ecole de Guerre. The young couple moved into a house on the Avenue de Trocadéro in Paris and Alfred Dreyfus set his sights on a position on the General Staff.

Dreyfus made no friends at the Ecole de Guerre. An unwritten law decreed that there should be no social mixing between the "proper" students and the "outsiders" and Dreyfus's personality tempted no one to break that law. A man of medium height, with high, broad shoulders, thinning light brown hair, pince-nez glasses and a small mustache, Dreyfus carried himself stiffly and made it clear by his bearing that he took enormous pride in the uniform and the insignia of rank that he wore. He gave an impression of overbearing self-assurance and he spoke in a reedy, toneless voice that unfailingly irritated his listeners. Ignoring the opportunities for a life of culture and gaiety that abounded in the beautiful city around him, he riveted his attention on his army career and his family — his wife, Lucie, and their son, Pierre, born a year after their marriage. He was undismayed by the reputation he had acquired of being a pompous bore who wrapped himself so tightly in the image of a military man that he appeared ridiculous. At thirty-three he had already overcome many obstacles on his path to success in the Army and he was still on the way up. That he had no friends among his fellow students didn't bother him. He had his work and his family. He cared for nothing else.

When, in 1893, Colonel Sandherr of the Statistical Section heard that a Jew was among the top twelve men in the graduating class at the Ecole de Guerre and was about to receive an appointment to the General Staff as a probationer, he tried to block the appointment and failed. Dreyfus went first to the General Staff's First Bureau which handled Army Administration and after six months there he was posted to the Fourth Bureau, Military Transportation. Next, he went to the Second Bureau, Army Intelligence (where Colonel Sandherr's request to keep him out of the Statistical Section was respected) and in 1894, at the time of the receipt of the bordereau, Dreyfus was serving with the Third Bureau in Operations and Training. He thought that all was going as well for him as could possibly be expected. His home life was serene; Lucie had given birth to a daughter, Jeanne, in 1893 and Dreyfus was well pleased with his family. He and Lucie often discussed their children's upbringing and made elaborate plans for their future. No word of the bordereau excitement seeped down to Dreyfus and, though he was mildly surprised, he was not alarmed when he received an order to report to the Ministry of War at nine o'clock on the morning of October 15, 1894, for a general inspection.

Arriving promptly at the War Ministry at the hour indicated, Dreyfus was received by Major Du Paty de Clam, a foppish little officer addicted to dramatic and flamboyant behavior. Three men dressed in civilian clothes, strangers to Dreyfus, were also present. Du Paty announced that he had injured his hand and would, therefore, ask Captain Dreyfus to be kind enough to write out a letter for him. It seemed to Dreyfus to be an odd request but he sat down at a desk, took pen in hand and, as the Major dictated, he wrote what appeared to be a routine letter concerned with military matters. Actually, Du Paty had loaded the text of the letter with phrases used in the bordereau and, as he strutted back and forth in front of Dreyfus, he carefully observed the captain's facial expression and general demeanor. After dictating the words, "a note on the hydraulic brake of the 120mm. gun," Du Paty stopped abruptly and, in a loud voice, demanded that Dreyfus explain why his hand trembled. Dreyfus replied that he had been unaware that his hand had trembled and that perhaps the tremor was due to the fact that his fingers were cold. He was surprised to note that his reply seemed to strike the major as impertinent but when Du Paty resumed dictating, he calmly went back to writing. All at once Du Paty threw all pretense aside. At the top of his voice he exclaimed, "I arrest you in the name of the law. You are accused of high treason!" As one of the three civilians walked over to his side, Dreyfus suddenly realized that the strangers were policemen. Aghast, he protested that he had committed no crime and demanded to see evidence against him. Brushing aside his protests, Du Paty merely replied that the War Office had overwhelming proof of his guilt and, as Dreyfus watched in horror, Du Paty placed a revolver on the desk in front of him. Now in a towering rage, Dreyfus shouted that he would certainly not kill himself but would instead take great care to live in order to prove his innocence. He took the keys to his house from his pocket and slapped them on the table. "Take these," he said, "and search my house. You will find nothing. I am innocent of any crime." Coldly, Major Du Paty informed Dreyfus that he would be taken to the Cherche-Midi military prison at once.

While the dramatic confrontation was taking place, Major Henry was waiting in the next room. His leave over, he had returned to the Statistical Section in the midst of the furor over the bordereau and, upon being briefed on all that had transpired in his absence, he cursed his luck. It had seemed to him then that all his hopes of playing a starring role in the apprehension of the traitor were dashed. But now, as he listened through a partially opened door to the proceedings in the next room, he thought he saw a way of getting himself back into the center of things. He took careful notes on his "impressions" of what he heard.

It had been prearranged that if Dreyfus did not cooperate by taking his own life, Major Henry would escort him to prison, and when Henry heard Du Paty place Dreyfus under arrest he presented himself in the next room. In the carriage en route to the Cherche-Midi, Henry pretended that he knew nothing of the matter at hand and asked Dreyfus of what he was accused. When, shaking with anger, Dreyfus answered that the charge was treason and that he had committed no crime of any kind, Henry told him to rest assured that if he was innocent his innocence would be recognized.

While Dreyfus was being taken to the Cherche-Midi, Du Paty and another officer hurried to search Dreyfus's home on the Avenue du Trocadéro. They would tell Madame

Dreyfus nothing but that her husband was being held on a very serious charge and that if she wished to help him and her country, she must say nothing about it to anyone until she received permission to do so. "A word, a single word from you and your husband is irretrievably lost," Du Paty told her. Terror-stricken, the young woman watched the two officers search through her husband's papers. Du Paty was counting on finding supporting evidence of Dreyfus's guilt — hopefully, some sheets of the same onion-skin paper on which the bordereau had been written, or, failing that, financial statements or an accumulation of bills that would indicate an urgent need of money. He found nothing. Dreyfus's affairs were in perfect order and his bankbook showed an impressive and obviously more than adequate balance.

At the Cherche-Midi, Lieutenant Colonel Forzinetti, the director of the prison, was seriously concerned over the behavior of his new prisoner. The man screamed, wept, beat his fists against the stone walls of his cell and threw himself bodily against its barred door. The corridors of the ancient jail rang with his anguished cries. "I am innocent," Dreyfus shouted again and again. "I am innocent. As God is my witness, I am innocent." Forzinetti's charges did not usually act in anything approaching this manner and he feared that the man was either mad or on the brink of insanity. It also occurred to him that Dreyfus might actually be innocent; if that were so, it would account for his bizarre behavior. The prison director went to Dreyfus's cell and questioned him and, as he listened to the frenzied man's tale of what had happened to him, it seemed to him that Dreyfus's indignation, worry and despondency were the entirely natural reactions of a man who had been unjustly accused. Slowly the conviction grew on Forzinetti that a serious error had been made.

On orders from General Mercier, news of Dreyfus's arrest was withheld from the press and Major Forzinetti was instructed to keep the identity of his new prisoner a carefully guarded secret. Dreyfus, himself, was kept in the dark about the exact nature of the charges against him for two weeks and then, when the bordereau was at last shown to him and he was told that the War Office was certain that he had written it, no one but Forzinetti paid any attention to his protestations that he had never even seen the document before. Dreyfus's despair grew with each passing day and just when Forzinetti was certain that at any moment his prisoner would burst the bounds of sanity, Major Du Paty came to interrogate him.

Du Paty was a small dandy of a man who affected a monocle and a waxed mustache and his whole demeanor announced to the world that he was a Marquis, the proud scion of a distinguished old French family. He thoroughly enjoyed the drama of the traitor hunt and he was confident that he would be able to extract a confession from the accused man. On his first visit he tried to charm his way into Dreyfus's confidence, but when his charm got him no more than repeated avowals of innocence, he decided to resort to more heroic measures. On subsequent visits he arrived at the Cherche-Midi in the dead of night, sent for Forzinetti and ordered the prison commandant to show him to Dreyfus's cell and stealthily unlock its door that he might surprise the prisoner in his sleep. Then, waking Dreyfus abruptly, he would hand the sleep-dazed man paper and pen and order him to take dictation, first in one position and then in another. "Stand up and write," Du Paty ordered. "Now, sit with one leg

crossed over the other and write leaning on your knee . . .
Now crouch and write the words I give you." His monocle
gleaming in the candlelight, Du Paty peered anxiously at the
results. Incredibly, he was hoping to surprise Dreyfus in
the posture he had assumed in order to disguise his handwriting while writing the bordereau. It was all to no avail;
Dreyfus's handwriting stubbornly continued to slant in
another direction than that of the bordereau.

Du Paty had one more trick up his sleeve. He returned to
the prison one day bringing with him a photograph of the
bordereau and photographs of letters Dreyfus had written.
He cut up all the photographs into small pieces, jumbled
the pieces together in a hat, and ordered Dreyfus to pick out
the scraps of his own handwriting. When Dreyfus unfailingly
avoided the fragments of bordereau writing, Du Paty spat
out his annoyance and left. During the next days, as Dreyfus's gloom deepened, Forzinetti wished that Du Paty would
come back. The prisoner's forced participation in the little
major's ludicrous games had served, at least, to distract him
from his anguish.

In the meantime, General Mercier's men were conducting
a frantic search for supporting evidence of Dreyfus's guilt
that would stand up in court. Proof of a secret liaison with
an expensive mistress would do; sworn testimony that
Dreyfus was seen often at gambling casinos would do;
evidence of personal business matters gone suddenly awry
would do. Nothing was found. Dreyfus's personal life was
discovered to be blameless; it wasn't even interesting.
More and more it looked as though General Mercier would
have to let Dreyfus go; a man couldn't be held indefinitely
without being brought to trial.

And then, all at once, the die was cast. A small item appeared in the November 1 edition of *La Libre Parole* under the headline of HIGH TREASON! ARREST OF A JEWISH OFFICER, CAPTAIN DREYFUS. The article stated that the prisoner had confessed, that the War Office had proof of his guilt and that the case would be hushed up because Dreyfus was a Jew. Somehow, in spite of all the feverish attempts to ensure secrecy, word of Dreyfus's arrest had leaked out. Reading the text of the news item, Mercier saw his worst fears realized. The article clearly implied that "Jewish money" had bought the War Minister's silence.

The rest of the Paris press pounced on the story without bothering to check on its accuracy and before long all of France was speculating on the horrifying tale of a confessed traitor basking in the protection of a bribed Minister of War. Mercier saw that he was stuck with his suspect. If Dreyfus were released now there would be no end to the stories in the press about the War Minister's having sold him his freedom and Mercier would be forced to resign. A hurried meeting of the Cabinet of Ministers was held. Mercier assured the meeting that he was certain of Dreyfus's guilt and, having no reason to doubt Mercier's word, the other Ministers joined him in a unanimous vote to prosecute.

4

The Jews of Europe

AT THE Cherche-Midi, Dreyfus was informed that he would be tried at a military court-martial. He stared through the bars of his cell in disbelief. A court-martial! He, who put his love for the Army on a par with his love for his family, tried at a court-martial! Lying on his cot and staring up at the ceiling of his cell, Dreyfus told himself again and again that a fantastic error had been made, that he was the victim of a tragic misunderstanding. Surely, as soon as the top men in the Army were acquainted with the true facts of his case his nightmare would be over.

It was true that Dreyfus was the victim of a tragic misunderstanding, but it involved far more than the misinterpretation of a set of circumstances that seemed to link him to the bordereau. If Dreyfus had not been a Jew, a name that started with the same initial von Schwartzkoppen had used to refer to his French contact, combined with a handwriting similar to that of the bordereau and a military background that could have given him knowledge of the matters it referred to, would not have been enough to send him to prison. If Dreyfus had not been a Jew, the news that he was being held in the Cherche-Midi would not have caused such a great sensation in the anti-Republic press. If Dreyfus had not been a Jew, Mercier might have dared to release him when the evidence against him proved to be insufficient.

Dreyfus, like many French Jews at the time, believed that assimilation would be the final answer to anti-Semitism and he was willing to forget the injustices done to the Jews in the past; he would have been content to live and let live had he been allowed to do so. He did not realize that the past, far from dead, was still to be reckoned with. Uncomprehending, he did not see that while a thickening fog of ancient myths about the Jews blinded the French people to his innocence, ghosts of an era that counted the rights of the individual as nothing against those of society were rising from the grave to draw France, beautiful, modern, enlightened France, back under the dark shadows of the Middle Ages.

Jews had been barred from France for three hundred years before the Great Revolution and all over Europe they had been reviled and persecuted since the rise of Christianity. As "unbelievers" they were considered to be a threat to all Christians and contact with them was discouraged by the early Catholic Church, which pronounced them to be inferior people and not entitled to the same rights as Christians. From on high came the word that "Jewish magic" was responsible for such natural disasters as earthquakes and epidemics, and the Jewish people, as "Christ-killers," were barred from public office and landownership and were ordered by the Church to wear an identifying badge. In those dark days Christians believed that it was God's will that Jews should live in misery. Jewish property was confiscated periodically and, without qualms of conscience, early Christians made the stoning of Jews a regular part of Holy Week. The Vatican drew the line at murder and torture. It was officially announced that the Jews had a right to exist.

It was in those times that Jews became "rootless wanderers." Finding temporary sanctuary in one land, they remained until persecution or an expulsion decree forced their flight to another. Often, groups of Jews did not wait to be expelled but moved on to other countries on the slim hope of finding a better life, leaving behind others, often members of their own families, who were not so hopeful.

In the gathering gloom of the Middle Ages, the lot of the Jews worsened. Barred not only from landownership but also from all artisan and commercial guilds, they sought their livelihoods in the only fields of endeavor open to them — usury, the lending of money at interest, and trade in second-hand goods. To ply their money trades, Jews followed their customers to the big commercial cities where they were forced to live in restricted areas — ghettos especially set aside for Jews. Surrounded by high walls that underlined and enforced their separation from the rest of society, Jews learned fear and suspicion of all Christians. As the outer city expanded outward to accommodate its growing population, the ghetto, restricted by its confining walls, grew upward in order to house its new generations. In the narrow streets, cut off by the high wooden buildings from the sun, bearded Jews with their ringleted sons, hurried to the synagogues to study the Torah and to find release from the woes of living in a world that hated Jews.

The emancipation of the Jews began with a changing concept of money. In the Middle Ages money was generally considered to be good for only one thing — the purchase of land. Land was wealth. Land was security. The Jews, however, forbidden to own land and always mindful of the fact that property of any kind could be taken away from them at the whim of a prince, saw money differently. To them, money was something to be loaned for a price or to be used as bribes to buy short respites from harassment. As a result, they grew accustomed to manipulating money. When, in the seventeenth and eighteenth centuries, the great feudal cities were gradually absorbed into rising nation-states, the new monarchs suddenly needed large amounts of ready cash for the expansion and consolidation of their holdings and they found that the Jews were the only ones who could or would supply it. Dealing commonly with money, the Jews had access to large sums and, used as they were to lending money, they, unlike their Christian neighbors, were willing to take the risks inherent in backing the monarchs' financial ventures. Thus, with the changing times, some Jews assumed an important role in the economies of the new states. In return for their loans, the Jews who made them were awarded certain privileges, privileges which allowed them to live considerably better than they had in the past. At first there were just a few of these "privileged" Jews who financed the states' business but, as the monarchs' need for credit grew, the resources of more and more Jews were called upon and gradually there emerged in many European countries, a class of wealthy "Court Jews" who lived on a higher scale than that of most of their Christian countrymen. These wealthy Jews, however, never accounted for more than a small fraction of their states' Jewish populations whose lot, on the whole, continued to be misery, poverty and degradation.

Still later, around the time of the French Revolution, "Court Jews" had to call on their family contacts in other countries in order to satisfy their monarchs' voracious hunger for credit. It was at that time that the Rothschild family emerged into international prominence. The saga of this family demonstrates how access to large sums of money and inter-European family ties could, in those days, be transformed into awesome power and enormous wealth.

Meyer Rothschild, a Jew who lived in the ghetto of Frankfort, Germany, operated a money-exchange house which became widely known for its success in investing the money of an Austrian nobleman. Soon Rothschild counted several royal families among his customers and he grew so rich that he was able to set up each of his five sons in his own banking house. With careful calculation he kept his oldest son in Frankfort to run the family business there and sent the other four sons to establish branches in Austria, England, Italy and France. This family of father and five sons had an amazing talent for the handling of money and, it seemed, an insatiable desire to amass more and more wealth. The banks run by the five Rothschild sons grew so powerful that, singly or in combination, they were able, by granting or refusing loans, to control whether or not wars would be launched and whether or not, once launched, they would be won.

The Rothschilds were unique. No other banking house, Christian or Jewish, ever approached them in wealth or power. No other Jewish family ever rivaled them for inter-European financial connections. And yet, because of the Rothschilds' storied wealth, people all over Europe, many of them people who had never even seen a Jew, thought of all Jews as rich. At a time when Europe was falling sick with the new virus of nationalism, all Jews were identified with the "statelessness" and "internationalism" of the Rothschilds. Soon after the French Revolution, the Rothschilds, while retaining their wealth undiminished, loosened their hold on the political strings of Europe, but because of this family's former political power, all Jews were firmly connected in the public mind with political intrigue.

The spread of the revolutionary spirit completed the political emancipation of the Jews. Liberty! Equality! Fraternity! The cry of the French Revolution rang throughout Europe and gradually most of Western and Central Europe's Jews were allowed to emerge from their ghettos into the sunlight of a world that had started to shake off its feudal bonds. France was the first European country to grant political equality to Jews and, for the first time in three hundred years, Jews came to France to live. Many of them tried to forget the past and to plunge themselves into the society which now seemed to welcome them. For a time they succeeded in doing just that. In the upper levels of society Jews mingled freely with Christians during the reigns of Napoleon I, Louis Philippe and Napoleon II. There was even considerable intermarriage between Jewish and Christian families. By the time of Louis Philippe it could be said that no serious anti-Semitism existed in France.

Then, in the 1890's, when the Tsar of Russia started a massive series of brutal anti-Semitic pogroms, thousands of Russian Jews fled westward seeking refuge and many of them ended up in France. These people were hard for Frenchmen, both Christian and Jewish, to take. They seemed to come directly from the Middle Ages. Their clothes, their mannerisms and their attitudes were those of a people long cut off from the rest of society; these "newcomer Jews" were suspicious and resentful of all Christians and many of them were characterized by the unscrupulousness of people long preoccupied with the problem of mere survival, people dominated by fear and insecurity.

Close on the heels of the Russian pogroms came the plague of French financial scandals. There were Jews involved in many of them and Christians involved in all of them. With the Panama Canal Affair, however, the anti-Semitic press loudly proclaimed that the Jews as a whole were responsible for the disgraceful corruption which de Lesseps's two Jewish "middlemen" actually shared with dozens of highly placed Christians.

And so it was that in the 1890's Frenchmen, fearful of Germany, distrustful of their own Republic, and morbidly afraid of betrayal from within, cast about for a scapegoat on which to blame their troubles and found that the Jews filled the bill admirably. Accounting for only .002 of the French population, they were powerless; endowed by their history with the reputation of being "rootless wanderers," they could be scorned as "not really French" by Frenchmen whose families had tilled the same soil for generations; having, as a result of past persecutions and expulsions, family connections scattered throughout Europe, they could be accused of having "divided loyalties"; identified with the opulent Rothschilds, they could be thought to possess a mysterious and sinister power over money matters. Over all these convenient stereotypes about the Jews, Frenchmen spread the conscience-salving unguent of church sanction for anti-Semitism; in Church schools French children were still taught that the Jews, as a people, were responsible for the death of Jesus Christ.

Alfred Dreyfus thought of himself, primarily, as a Frenchman and an Army officer and only incidentally as a Jew, and in his cell in the Cherche-Midi he clung to the belief that he was the victim of a terrible error which his superiors in the Army would soon find out and rectify. But, on the Rue St. Dauphine, General Mercier, pressured by an unbridled anti-Republic and anti-Semitic press, was convinced that only through Dreyfus's conviction as a traitor could he save his own skin. He sent word to the Statistical Section that he must have a strong case to present to the court-martial judges. Accordingly, Colonel Sandherr directed Major Henry to go through the Section's files and to collect everything that might have a bearing on the Dreyfus matter. Henry did more than that. He made up a dossier on Dreyfus which included not only those papers which might, with the help of an elastic imagination, legitimately be thought to incriminate Dreyfus, but also several documents of doubtful authenticity. No one of these last could stand up under a careful scrutiny but, when seen together with the bordereau and such wastebasket scraps as the "Scoundrel D." memorandum, they presented an ominous overall picture of treachery pointing dramatically to Alfred Dreyfus.

5

Court-Martial

WHILE Dreyfus waited in the Cherche-Midi for his court-martial trial to begin, he was tried and convicted in the anti-Republic "nationalist" press. Newspapers that spoke for Monarchist and Bonapartist factions assumed his guilt and, deploring the Republic's failure to guard the nation's security, pointed out to their readers that had Dreyfus's treachery gone undetected, his position on the General Staff would have enabled him, in the event of a war, to conspire with enemy powers to send their sons straight into death-traps. Clerical journals representing Catholic groups that disagreed with Pope Leo XIII's policy of "adjustment" to republican governments seized on the Dreyfus matter as a means of attacking the French Republic. In the hopes of spurring a movement to restore the French Church to its pre-Revolution position of political power these Catholic papers enthusiastically joined the Anti-Semitic chorus led by *La Libre Parole;* one of them, *La Croix,* the official organ of the Assumptionist order, announced that Dreyfus was a paid agent of an international Jewish conspiracy that aimed to ruin the French people and take over the territory of France.

Even normally conservative editors allowed themselves to be caught up in the spy fever. One "discovered" a beautiful Italian woman who had blackmailed Dreyfus into betraying

his country. Another, either not knowing or not caring that
Dreyfus had never been to Russia, "disclosed" the name
of the hotel he had stayed at when he had gone to St. Peters-
burg "to confer with German aristocrats." Each day a fresh
crop of rumors crowded the few available facts out of the
headlines; when there was a dearth of genuine rumors newspapermen supplied the lack by concocting a new batch out
of their heads. More than a dozen newspapers were printed
in Paris in those days and each was in stiff competition with
the others for readers; high journalistic ideals and a fine dis-
regard for profit were needed to resist the temptation to
print the hodgepodge of half-truths, lies and wild improvisa-
tions that sold the most papers.

At first General Mercier was castigated almost as sharply
as was Dreyfus himself. The general's attempt to suppress
news of Dreyfus's arrest was widely interpreted as evidence
that he had been bribed by Dreyfus's friends. When he tried
to stem the tide of sensational newspaper stories by publicly
announcing that the documents involved in the Dreyfus Case
were "of small importance," he accomplished nothing more
than to get himself more deeply embroiled in the snowballing wild speculation. Mercier, the press reported, had
been paid by a "Jewish Syndicate" to play down the significance of the secrets that had been sold to enemy agents.
When, however, it was learned that the Cabinet had voted
to prosecute Dreyfus, the newspapers changed their tune.
All at once, Frenchmen heard that the Jewish Syndicate had
met its match in the "valiant" General Mercier who had in
his possession "overwhelming proof" of Dreyfus's guilt. One
paper quoted the general as saying that Dreyfus had been
in contact with a foreign government for three years and
the next day another paper printed Mercier's denial of the

story. Nobody paid any attention to the denial. The average Frenchman had little enough excitement in his life and, having gotten his teeth into a story of espionage and high intrigue that promised just retribution for a dastardly spy, he was not going to let facts or denials make him loosen his hold.

On November 2, the day after the public learned of Dreyfus's arrest, the French Foreign Office intercepted and, after considerable difficulty, decoded a telegram sent by Panizzardi, the Italian military attaché in Paris, to his headquarters in Rome. "If Captain Dreyfus has not had relations with you, it would be well to order the Ambassador to publish an official denial, in order to avoid press comment," the message read. What significance did this telegram have? The French Foreign Office decided that since the telegram was sent in a code that was so hard to break, it almost certainly reflected its sender's true sentiments; Panizzardi must have been genuinely puzzled by the talk in the French press of Dreyfus's connections with "foreigners" and, with his telegram, he must have been checking to see if Dreyfus had been dealing with Rome without his, Panizzardi's, knowledge. Seen in that light, Panizzardi's message seemed to lend credence to Dreyfus's protestations of innocence. Yet, in the course of events, the text of this telegram, altered to suit the purposes of the War Office, would be handed secretly from one military hand to another and would be used time and again as a powerful weapon against Dreyfus.

Sixteen days after Dreyfus's arrest and one day before news of it appeared in the press, Madame Lucie Dreyfus was permitted to notify her husband's family of his plight. One of his brothers, Mathieu Dreyfus, hurried to Paris in high indignation, determined to force a prompt rectification of what he was sure was a monstrous error. On applying to Army authorities, however, Mathieu was told that he could not even see the prisoner, that vital national interests were at stake and that he could serve his brother best by patiently waiting for developments. Mathieu, a small, distinguished-looking man, seethed with impatience and busied himself with finding a competent lawyer to represent his brother at the court-martial. He approached one of the most noted attorneys in Paris, Edgar Demange, a devout Catholic with a brilliant record of courtroom victories and an impeccable reputation in the legal world. Demange, middle-aged, portly and impressively bearded, hesitated before giving Mathieu his answer. He knew that public passions had been so aroused on the subject of Alfred Dreyfus that any lawyer undertaking his defense would be subject to bitter attack. Could he risk his whole career for the sake of a man, a Jew, who might have been unjustly accused? Moved by the story Mathieu Dreyfus had told him, and excited by the challenge of the case, Demange found that he could — under certain conditions. He made it clear to Mathieu that he would defend his brother only if, after interviewing him and examining the evidence against him, he was convinced of his innocence. On the other hand, he warned Mathieu, if he found himself unconvinced, he would publicly refuse the case.

On December 5, the military authorities allowed Demange to examine a photograph of the bordereau and, on the same day, the lawyer went to see Alfred Dreyfus at the Cherche-Midi. Later, declaring himself satisfied as to the accused man's innocence, he announced that he would be the lawyer for the defense. Dreyfus took heart and, on the eve of his trial, he wrote to Lucie:

Ma bonne cherie,

At last I am approaching the end of my sufferings, the end of my torture. Tomorrow I shall appear before my judges, my head held high, my soul at peace . . . I am ready to stand before my fellow soldiers as a soldier who has nothing for which to reproach himself. My innocence they will see in my face, read in my eyes . . . You may sleep peacefully, my dear, you need have no anxiety. Think only of our joy at being so soon in one another's arms again.

The trial opened on December 19, 1894, in an ancient palace on the Rue Cherche-Midi across the street from the prison. Because some newspapers had announced that the trial would be closed to spectators, the general public stayed away and the audience was composed mainly of newspaper reporters. In the front of the gloomy, gaslit courtroom, seven high-ranking Army officers, splendid in full-dress uniforms, sat as the court-martial judges. Also present were the Deputy Chief of the General Staff, General Charles Gonse, Major Du Paty and, acting as official observer for General Mercier, Major Georges Picquart. Mathieu Dreyfus was there but Lucie was not; Alfred had begged her not to come to his trial. "Save your strength," he had written to her. "We shall need all our united strength to care for each other, to help each other to forget this terrible trial."

When all was in readiness Dreyfus, himself, was brought in. Wearing the uniform of a General Staff officer, he walked stiffly to the chair set aside for the accused. As he glanced around he appeared to be pleased by the presence of so many important officers and he replied calmly to the opening questions about his name and rank. His thin, toneless voice, however, startled those who had never heard him speak and its grating quality rang harshly in the tense, quiet courtroom.

Demange immediately tried to establish that the bordereau was the only real evidence the prosecution could use against Dreyfus. The newspapers had told the public of the existence of "overwhelming proof" of Dreyfus's guilt and Demange wanted to make it clear that this "proof" consisted of no more than one document which actually proved nothing. But before he could accomplish his objective, the government succeeded in having the trial declared secret and the newspapermen, whom Demange had hoped would carry the story of an unjustly accused man to the public, were ordered to leave the courtroom. Mathieu, too, had to leave; only those involved in the case and the official observers were allowed to remain. In spite of what was obviously a serious setback, Dreyfus's expression did not change. For the sake of his reputation he would have preferred to have his vindication come in public but, since his military superiors had ordered otherwise, he would be content with an acquittal arrived at in secret.

The trial started. The judges heard Dreyfus categorically deny the charges of treason. Then the witnesses for the prosecution and for the defense were heard. Taking the witness stand, Major Henry reported at length on his impressions of Dreyfus's behavior on the day when he was accused by Major Du Paty; it seemed to him, Henry said, that Dreyfus had acted like a guilty man. Major Du Paty dramatically elaborated on the scene Henry had described; the prisoner's hand, Du Paty said, had trembled visibly when certain words taken from the text of the bordereau were dictated. Next, character witnesses for Dreyfus — a few Army officers and the Chief Rabbi of Paris — testified to his spotless reputation. At the end of the first day of the trial, it appeared that the prosecution's case could be based on no more than opinion and a document that could not be definitely linked to the accused man. Major Picquart reported to General Mercier that no court could possibly convict on the evidence the judges had before them.

General Mercier was in very hot water. Sure that an acquittal for Dreyfus would deal a mortal blow to his career, he pressed the Statistical Section to produce definitive evidence of Dreyfus's guilt. Colonel Sandherr saw his own job as tied up with Mercier's — a new Minister of War would certainly want to make a clean sweep of a counterespionage service that had allowed a traitor to escape undetected — and Major Henry, whose carefully laid plans to ensure his eventual succession to Colonel Sandherr's position had gone awry, still had hopes of salvaging some prestige and advancement from the "traitor matter." The two officers conferred and then assured General Mercier that they had a file on Dreyfus which would prove helpful. Henry added that if he could take the stand again he could help the judges to see Dreyfus's guilt.

Early on the second day of the trial, Henry asked to be recalled. He told the judges that the Statistical Section had long suspected that an officer on the General Staff was selling military secrets to a foreign power and, he added, one of the Section's informants had actually told him the traitor's name. Suddenly, Henry pointed to Dreyfus and shouted, "There is the traitor!" Shaken from his composure, Dreyfus jumped to his feet and loudly demanded that the court call Henry's informant. Henry, however, refused to give the man's name, implying that if he did national security would be dangerously threatened. The presiding judge, impressed by the plea of "reasons of state," asked Henry if he would at least swear that the unnamed individual had said that the traitor was Dreyfus. Henry raised his right hand and said, "I swear it."

On the third day, Bertillon was called to testify on the question of handwriting. He drew complicated diagrams on a blackboard and expounded at great length on the mathematical equations he had used in arriving at his conclusions. The judges stared at him blankly; his prattle sounded like a madman's. Bertillon was able, however, to get across to the judges what his bizarre conclusions were: Dreyfus had written the bordereau but in so doing he had disguised his handwriting by copying the handwriting characteristics of his wife and of his brother.

Still it seemed that the court must acquit. Henry's testimony had been dramatic but he would not produce his informant to back it up. Bertillon's blackboard labyrinth was visually imposing but his conclusion was, after all, only an opinion and a conflicting one had been given by the expert from the Banque de France. Still conspicuously missing was a plausible motive for treachery. Dreyfus was comfortably off; his wife had a substantial family income of her own; there was no scandal connected with Dreyfus's name; his Army record was good. No, there was not yet enough reason to convict.

By the end of the fourth morning of the trial all the witnesses had been heard. As the judges rose to leave the courtroom for the luncheon recess, Major Du Paty approached the presiding judge and handed him an envelope containing the file on Dreyfus concocted by Henry and Sandherr. Du Paty whispered to the judge that the envelope held highly confidential material which must be returned to the War Minister immediately after the trial. In the judges' chamber the envelope was opened and its contents passed around.

The "secret file" contained a motley mixture of genuine clues, distortions, deliberate falsifications and hearsay. The judges saw not only the von Schwartzkoppen memos that referred to "the Scoundrel D." and "a dangerous situation for me with a French officer" but also a summary of Dreyfus's Army career that included several "facts" that were not facts and a translation of Panizzardi's telegram to his headquarters in Rome that bore little resemblance to the original message that the Foreign Office had so carefully decoded. The summary of Dreyfus's career stated that while at Bourges he had sold the secret of the French melanite shell to the Germans. The judges were shocked; they had known of the Germans' acquisition of this secret but they did not know that the French War Office had evidence that the Germans had acquired it sometime before Dreyfus had been posted to Bourges. Panizzardi's telegram, originally a straightforward request to his headquarters in Rome to deny French press reports of Italian contacts with Dreyfus if there were, in fact, none, now read: "Dreyfus arrested. Precautions taken. Emissary warned." All this material was wrapped in a batting of "hearsay papers" such as a verbal notation of the ex-spy's warning that "there is a traitor in your midst." And, lending authority and credence to the whole package, a covering note from the Minister of War strongly implied that the file the judges were examining had convinced him, Mercier, of Dreyfus's guilt.

In the course of their work for the Statistical Section, Major Henry and Colonel Sandherr had helped to manufacture hundreds of "documents" containing false information to be sold by counterspies to the Germans. Daily, they dealt with people of the murkiest backgrounds whose motives for spying for France were more often personal gain than patriotism. Responsible only to a Deputy Chief of Staff who preferred to be in the dark about what went on in the Statistical Section, Sandherr and Henry moved in a shadowy world of relative truths and lived by a special code that decreed right to be what was right for the Army and justified any means as long as it accomplished its end. Often their own interests and those of the Army conveniently coincided. Such was the case in the matter of the Dreyfus file. The Minister of War had been accused of "inefficiency" and thus the prestige of the whole Army and, incidentally, the War Minister's job, were at stake; the Minister of War needed proof of Dreyfus's guilt to shore up public confidence in the Army and, incidentally, to save his own skin; Sandherr and Henry were in a position to supply that proof. The Army's honor would be preserved and General Mercier, the Army's highest ranking officer, would be indebted to Colonel Sandherr and Major Henry. It didn't matter that the Dreyfus file was stuffed with half-truths and outright lies; if it convinced the judges, it was proof of his guilt.

Sandherr and Henry had done their work well. Impressed by the delicate nature of the papers they were examining, the judges were convinced that they were dealing with a matter involving national security. Unaware of the legerdemain that had produced it, they agreed that the file pointed inexorably to Dreyfus as the guilty man. The judges were all military men and no one of them had had legal training. If they knew that their consideration of evidence that had not been seen by the defense was strictly illegal, they managed to squelch their pangs of conscience — after all, the secret evidence had been sent to them by the Minister of War.

The court reconvened and the final pleas of the prosecuting

attorney and the attorney for the defense were heard. Demange spoke for three hours, concentrating his remarks on the bordereau which was, as far as he knew, the only evidence of any importance presented against Dreyfus. When he finally sat down he was sure that he had torn the prosecution's case to shreds. The attorney for the prosecution spoke briefly and when Dreyfus was asked if he had anything further to add, he stood up and said simply, "I am innocent."

The judges retired and, since it was the custom for the accused to be absent when the verdict was read, Dreyfus was taken to an adjoining room. After a brief interval, the seven judges returned and their verdict was read aloud. By a unanimous vote they had decided that Dreyfus was guilty of treason and they had passed the most severe sentence the law allowed — degradation, deportation and life-exile in a fortified place. The audience sat in stunned silence. Many had considered a verdict of guilty possible but no one had expected a unanimous decision. Thinking of the man waiting in the next room, Demange wept.

Dreyfus was informed of the verdict and taken back to his cell where he immediately tried to kill himself by dashing his head against the stone wall. Forzinetti was sent for and he pleaded with Dreyfus to take heart. He told the unhappy man that he, personally, believed wholeheartedly in his innocence and he argued that it was Dreyfus's duty to his wife and children to go on living since suicide would be seen as an admission of guilt. Finally, Dreyfus allowed himself to be convinced and the next day he wrote to Lucie:

> . . . My bitterness is such, my heart is so bruised, that I should already have got rid of this sad life if memory of you had not hindered me . . . I shall try to live for

your sake, but I have need of your aid . . . Above all
else, no matter what may become of me, search for the
truth; move Earth and Heaven to discover it; sink in
the effort, if need be, all our fortune, to rehabilitate
my name, which is now dragged through the mud. No
matter what may be the cost, we must wash out the
unmerited stain.

The secret file on Dreyfus was returned to the Statistical
Section with special instructions from General Mercier to
the effect that his covering note was to be destroyed and the
other papers were to be dispersed in the Section's regular
files. Sandherr and Henry disobeyed the General's orders.
They had saved Mercier's job in this matter but, politics
being what they were, he might lose it at any time on
another. A new Minister of War might be curious about the
background of the Dreyfus Case and if he were to ferret out
the illegality of the procedure that had been followed, it
would be best for the Statistical Section if the blame seemed
to fall on General Mercier alone. Sandherr and Henry put
all the documents seen by the judges in a separate folder
which they marked "Secret" and filed in a locked safe.

6

Degradation and Exile

JANUARY 5, 1895. The morning sky over Paris was leaden gray and a chill wind whistled around the corners of the city's streets and boulevards. Outside the great courtyard of the Ecole Militaire scores of people stamped their feet and thrust their hands deep in their coat pockets. A contingent of white-gloved gendarmes stood at the gate of the courtyard, shoulders hunched and chins tucked into overcoat collars. All at once the sound of marching feet was heard. Springing into position, the gendarmes stretched out their arms and held back the crowd which pressed behind them to watch as line after line of soldiers, a detachment from each of the garrisons stationed in Paris, paraded smartly into the courtyard and positioned themselves along its edges. More and more spectators arrived. The crowd grew, became a throng and then a mob. Pushing and jostling, the people jockeyed for the best positions from which to see over the shoulders of the gendarmes and the soldiers. Their mood was ferocious and exultant. They had come to see and hear what they could of the degradation of a traitor to France.

Were there no doubts in their minds about the guilt of the man they had come to see shamed? There were none. Seven high-ranking officers of the great French Army had, in one voice, proclaimed the fact of the man's treachery.

Would these men of the highest honor have acted so if the slightest shred of doubt remained? But of course they would not. They had got the right man. The only pity was that the law did not allow the judges to pass a more severe sentence. It was only right that a despicable traitor should be put to death.

The tower clock struck nine. A general on horseback rode to the center of the yard, raised his sword and shouted the command, "Shoulder arms!" The sound of gloved hands slapped on thousands of rifles was heard. There was a roll of drums and then silence. A flurry of snowflakes drifted down on the scene. The crowd held its breath. All at once a door in the corner of the courtyard opened and Dreyfus appeared, accompanied by four gunners. Head held high, sword in hand, gold braid gleaming at his cap and sleeve cuffs, Dreyfus strode forward with his escort. Shrill whistles and hoots rose from the crowd and then died down when the gendarmes gestured for quiet. The little group of marching men halted in front of the waiting general. With military precision the four gunners stepped back four paces, leaving Dreyfus standing alone and exposed. The general rose in his stirrups, pointed his sword to the sky and said, "Alfred Dreyfus, you are unworthy of your uniform. In the name of the French people we degrade you." Dreyfus stood motionless for a moment and then, flinging his arms high above his head, he shouted, "I am innocent. I swear I am innocent. Vive la France!" Outside the gate, the huge mob surged against the wall of the compound and answered him; a cry of "Death to the traitor!" rose from a thousand throats.

Dreyfus let his arms fall and stood at attention as an adjutant approached him. Slowly and methodically, the soldier ripped off the gold braid from the condemned man's cap and sleeves, tore the buttons off his tunic and shoulder straps and the insignia of rank off his collar and threw them all on the muddy ground. Next, the adjutant reached for Dreyfus's sword and, raising his knee, he broke the sword across it and flung the two pieces to the ground. Once again the tormented voice rose, thin and piercing, "In the name of my wife and children I swear that I am innocent. I swear it. Vive la France!" and once again the crowd spat out its hatred and contempt in a rising chorus of boos and hisses.

Then, as the habits of a sixteen-year-long military career asserted themselves over his anguish, Dreyfus straightened and, responding to a command, started to march with his escort around the courtyard. The prescribed ritual of degradation required him to parade his shame before the eyes of the assembled troops and, as he walked briskly along, it was obvious that he was determined to play the part demanded of him. His uniform was disheveled and loose threads hung from it where the braid and insignia had been ripped off but he carried his head high. Though a new outburst of hoots and catcalls broke from the mob as he passed the gate, he kept his eyes straight ahead. When he reached a small knot of newspapermen who stood taking notes on the scene, he paused in front of them. "You will say to the whole of France that I am innocent," he called out, but the reporters, intoxicated with the heady aroma of hatred that filled the air, answered him with cries of "Traitor!" "Coward!" "Dirty Jew!"

At the end of his tour, Dreyfus stood silent as he was handcuffed. Two gendarmes hustled him into a waiting prison van, the driver called out to the horses and the van rattled away. The commanding general raised his sword; drums rolled, bugles sounded, a military band struck up a lively tune and the troops marched out of the courtyard as the mob shouted again and again, "Death to the Jew!" "Death to the Jew!"

Dreyfus was held in Paris for two weeks during which time his wife was allowed to visit him twice. Then, hand-cuffed and ankles fettered, he was taken by train to a port on the western coast of France and from there to a temporary prison on an offshore island. Again Lucie was permitted to visit him but their meetings were agonizing for both husband and wife; a jailer stood between them and each time Lucie was sent away after half an hour. On the 21st of February, Lucie saw a ship lying at anchor in the harbor and, guessing that it would be on this ship that Dreyfus would sail to his exile, she begged the jailer for permission to embrace her husband in farewell. The permission was denied. That night Dreyfus was put aboard the *Saint-Nazaire* and locked in a cell in her forecastle. The temperature hovered near zero and an icy sea wind blew in off the decks. Alfred Dreyfus huddled in a corner of his cell and wept. The next morning, the *Saint-Nazaire* weighed anchor and steamed off in a southwesterly direction. Dreyfus called out to his guards, asking them where the ship was heading. No one answered him. No one spoke to him during the entire nineteen-day voyage.

When the ship's engines finally stopped, Dreyfus guessed from remarks he had heard passed among the guards that the ship had anchored at Royal Island, one of the three islands of the Salvation group which lay broiling under the tropical sun ten miles off the coast of French Guiana. For one month, Dreyfus was held in a barred and shuttered cell on Royal Island and then, on April 13, he was taken to Devil's Island, which had formerly been used as a lepers' colony and which had just been cleared and made ready for use as his prison. Devil's Island, a barren rock, four hundred yards wide and two miles long, had been designated as Alfred Dreyfus's world for the rest of his life.

A small stone hut had been built to house Dreyfus and his guards. It was divided into two sections by a door made of iron bars through which the guards on one side could keep a constant watch on Dreyfus on the other. Straight off, the prisoner was told the conditions under which he would have to live: by day, he would be permitted to walk about accompanied by an armed guard, within a clearly defined half-acre area; at dusk he would be locked into his section of the hut; he would have to sleep in the light of a lantern that would burn all night lest any sudden movement on his part escape the attention of his guard; if he did not wish to eat his food raw, he would have to cook it over a wood fire outside the hut; talking to the guards would do him no good — they would not answer; he would be allowed to write and receive letters but reference to his case in any but the most general terms would be forbidden; all incoming and outgoing letters would be read by the Minister of Colonies and, to make sure that he got no good from the use of a clever code that escaped the notice of the censor, some of the letters he wrote and some of those written to him would not go through at all. Here, on this desolate rock of Devil's Island, under these conditions, Alfred Dreyfus was supposed to live out the rest of his days.

During his second night on Devil's Island, Dreyfus rose from his cot and, by the light of the guard's lantern, he started a diary:

It is impossible for me to sleep. This cage before

which the guard walks up and down like a phantom
appearing in my dreams, the plague of insects which
run over my skin, the rage which is smothered in my
heart that I should be here, when I have always and
everywhere done my duty — all this overexcites my
nerves which are already shattered and drives away
sleep . . . Where are the beautiful dreams of my youth
and the aspirations of my manhood? My heart is dead
within me; my brain reels with the turmoil of my
thoughts. What is the mystery underlying this tragedy? Even now I understand nothing of what has
passed. To be condemned without palpable proofs,
on the strength of a bit of handwriting!

I open the blind which closes my little window and
look again upon the sea. The sky is full of great clouds,
but the moonlight filters through, tingeing the sea with
silver. The waves break powerless at the foot of the
rocks which outline the shape of the island. There
is a constant lapping of the water, as it plays upon the
beach with a rude staccato rhythm that soothes my
wounded soul.

And in the days that followed he wrote to Lucie. He spoke
of his torment and of his love for her and their children and,
again and again, he proposed the same bargain: he would
live — somehow, in spite of his grief and his pain, he would
live — if she would persevere faithfully and unremittingly
in an effort to find the true traitor. In love and in anguished
impatience, he wrote:

Let no setback rebuff you or discourage you. Search
out, if you think it useful, the members of the government, move their hearts, as fathers and as Frenchmen.
Tell them that you ask for me no mercy, no pity, but

only that the investigations may be absolutely thorough . . .

I suffer not for myself only, but yet more deeply for you, for our dear children. It is from them, my darling, that you must draw the moral strength, the superhuman energy which you need to succeed in making our honor appear again to every one, no matter at what price, what it has always been, pure and spotless . . . But I know you. I know the greatness of your soul. I have confidence in you.

Back in Paris, Lucie wept over her husband's letters and conferred with his brother, Mathieu. Of course they would do every last thing that it was in their power to do to obtain a review of Alfred's case. How could they possibly rest at night if they did not spend their waking hours in a ceaseless effort to right the terrible wrong that had been done? They wrote loving letters to Dreyfus, assuring him, over and over again, that he could depend on them. Lucie told the children, Pierre and Jeanne, that their father had been assigned to foreign duty and that, like good children of a good soldier, they must wait patiently for his return.

The days dragged past slowly on Devil's Island. The weather alternated monotonously between dry, stifling heat and torrential downpours. Carefully schooling himself to restrain his gnawing impatience, Dreyfus waited, sustained by the thought of his wife's and his brother's limitless devotion. He could not guess that the first fruitful moves toward his vindication would be taken, not by Lucie and Mathieu, but by a man he barely knew, a man who had always been as antipathetic to Jews as most Frenchmen, a man named Lieutenant Colonel Georges Picquart.

Section

II

CRACKS IN A CLOSED CASE

7

Lieutenant Colonel Georges Picquart

ON MARCH 15, 1896, when Dreyfus had been on Devil's Island a little more than a year, a French Intelligence agent removed an unstamped "petit bleu," a blue special delivery postcard, from the pocket of an overcoat hanging in the cloakroom of a Paris restaurant. The overcoat belonged to Colonel Max von Schwartzkoppen, who clearly intended to buy a stamp and mail the card on his way home from the restaurant. The man to whom the card was addressed never received it; it landed on the desk of the new Chief of the Statistical Section, Lieutenant Colonel Georges Picquart.

> Sir: I shall wait for a more detailed explanation of the question in hand than you gave me the other day. Please let me have it in writing so that I can judge whether to continue my relations with the firm of R. or not.
>
> C.

Picquart stared at the blue card on the desk in front of him, trying to fathom its meaning. Evidently, von Schwartzkoppen was issuing an ultimatum to one of his informants: Either produce something specific that I can use or I won't have anything further to do with you. The message itself didn't trouble Picquart. He knew of dozens of low characters who, stumbling on bits of valueless information, might try to convince von Schwartzkoppen that they had something worth buying. Such people, having no important contacts and, therefore, no access to confidential material, were considered by the Statistical Section to be beneath its notice. If the petit bleu had been addressed to such a person, Picquart would have torn it up and thrown it away. But it was not. The name on the address side of the card was Major Count Ferdinand Walsin-Esterhazy. What "question in hand" could there possibly be between the German military attaché and an officer in the French Army? Picquart ordered a complete security check placed on Major Esterhazy.

Picquart had been appointed Chief of the Statistical Section in the summer of 1895 when Colonel Sandherr, gravely ill, had been forced to give up his post. Major Henry, having cherished hopes of succeeding to Sandherr's position, was disgruntled and he told a friend in the Foreign Office that he missed Sandherr, that Picquart was a "bad egg" who drove the men under him too hard. But Henry's was a minority opinion; Picquart, a handsome man of forty-three, quiet, cultivated and highly intelligent, was widely admired and liked. The new Chief was unmarried and, though he affected a cool and rather distant manner, it was well known that he considered the Army to be his whole life and was passionately devoted to furthering its interests. It was true that under Picquart a new atmosphere prevailed in the Section; the Chief insisted on a general tightening up of previously slipshod procedure and, as a result, the work of the Section was carried on more smoothly and efficiently than it had been under Sandherr.

Shortly after assuming his new position, Picquart had received a visit from the Chief of the General Staff, General

Boisdeffre, and had learned that Boisdeffre was still troubled about the Dreyfus Case. "Of course the case is closed," the general had said to Picquart, "but there is one aspect of it that haunts me. What motive, I ask myself, could Dreyfus have had for treachery? The man had everything — wealth, a satisfactory family situation, a responsible position in the Army. What could have induced him to betray his country?" Boisdeffre had suggested to Picquart that he examine whatever material the Army had on Dreyfus; perhaps he could come up with a logical explanation.

Although Picquart had acted as an observer for General Mercier at Dreyfus's trial, he had not seen the contents of the secret file that Du Paty had given to the judges. The court-martial's verdict had surprised him — the evidence he had heard had not seemed to him to be sufficient to convict — but he had not thought to question it. Now, however, Boisdeffre's visit reminded him that just before Sandherr had left the Statistical Section he had shown him where the secret dossier on Dreyfus was kept. Picquart pulled it out of the files and, on examining its contents, was shocked to see the scanty and inconclusive nature of the evidence that had sent a man into exile and disgrace. He knew, as the lawyer Demange had known, that the bordereau alone was not enough to condemn Dreyfus and he recognized several of the papers in the dossier for what they were — documents whose authenticity could easily be called into question. Shaken by what he had seen, he returned the dossier to the files and said nothing. The Dreyfus Case, he reminded himself, was closed.

Yes, the case was closed. When newspaper headlines reported Dreyfus safely incarcerated on Devil's Island, Frenchmen everywhere breathed a sigh of relief. France was secure again; the traitor had been found out, convicted and sent to his punishment. Overnight all talk of the case dried up; it seemed that all of France was anxious to forget that a man named Alfred Dreyfus had ever existed.

Everywhere that Lucie and Mathieu Dreyfus turned in their efforts to force a review of the case, they ran up against a stone wall. No, they were told, there was no point in discussing it further — unless, of course, some new fact could be found to prove Dreyfus's innocence. Well, could they, then, look at the bordereau, the document that had been used to convict him, in order that they might have a starting point from which to look for such proof? No, that was out of the question; the bordereau was top secret, far too delicate a document to be allowed out of the hands of the military. Refusing to give up, Mathieu had those facts of the case that were publicly known, together with the contradictions they contained, printed in a small pamphlet which he sent to influential Frenchmen whom he thought might help him. The pamphlet brought no tangible results; a few close friends privately encouraged him to continue his search for the real traitor but that was all. Doggedly, Mathieu and Lucie stuck to the course they had set for themselves. They wrote letters to government officials and military authorities; they petitioned; they pleaded. It became known all over France that the traitor's wife and brother were still hoping to clear his name; their devotion to a man so low that he would sell his country was considered to be naïve and foolish but, after all, rather touching as well.

By January of 1895, before Dreyfus had even sailed to his exile, General Mercier, who had clung so tenaciously and at such expense to Dreyfus to his job as Minister of War, was out of it. A dispute over the granting of railroad franchises had led to the resignation of not only the Premier and his Cabinet but the President of France as well. The new President, Félix Faure, had trouble keeping a Premier; the first one he appointed fell after ten months and his successor's hold on his job was shaky at best. Neither Premier considered Mercier for the War Ministry; each thought him too "controversial." His name was connected with the Dreyfus Case and throughout the government it was believed that it would be best for France if the Dreyfus Case were forgotten.

Forgotten. Yes, Colonel Picquart told himself, the Dreyfus Case should be forgotten. But, since March 15, 1896, the day that the petit bleu addressed to Major Esterhazy was placed on his desk, Picquart could not forget. He had already been troubled for some time by the knowledge that in spite of Dreyfus's deportation, military documents were still disappearing from the Army's files and, on seeing the petit bleu, it occurred to him that Esterhazy might be the man responsible. Perhaps, he speculated, Esterhazy had worked with Dreyfus for the Germans; if so, there was still another traitor in the French Army to be unmasked. Anxiously, Picquart waited for the results of Esterhazy's security check and when, finally, they came in, his suspicions were redoubled. His agents told him that Esterhazy was a rogue and a blackguard who led a debauched life revolving around wine, women and the pursuit of money. He borrowed where he could, made ill-advised plunges in the stock market and then tried to recoup his losses in the gambling casinos where he invariably fell deeper into debt. Though his combat record had been good, his behavior since the war had been distinctly erratic and unreliable and an officer of the regiment he was currently serving with reported that Esterhazy paid far too little attention to his duties and showed an abnormal interest in learning confidential information on guns and gunnery.

Picquart felt that he must confide his suspicions to General Boisdeffre. He showed the general the petit bleu, told him the results of his agents' investigations of Esterhazy, and said that he thought he had turned up another traitor. Boisdeffre agreed that the picture looked black for Esterhazy but added that he feared "starting another Dreyfus Case." He assured Picquart that Esterhazy would be gotten rid of, would be put on retired pay and, without any scandal, would be put in a position where he could do no further harm.

And so it might have turned out had it not been for the intervention of Esterhazy himself. In August, 1896, knowing nothing of Picquart's suspicions, Esterhazy wrote several letters of application for a post on the General Staff and these came to Picquart's attention. Such letters from a man of Esterhazy's reputation seemed to Picquart to be the height of impudence — unless, he reflected, the man actually was a German agent and, desperate for money, was seeking access to confidential information to sell to von Schwartzkoppen. Suddenly, Picquart was struck by how familiar Esterhazy's handwriting seemed. All at once he remembered what it reminded him of. He went to the files and pulled out the bordereau. When he placed the document next to Esterhazy's letters, it seemed to him that the handwritings were identical. To back up his judgment, he masked out the signatures, dates and identifying phrases in Esterhazy's letters, had the letters photographed and showed the photographs to Bertillon. Without a moment's hesitation, Bertillon said, "Ah, the handwriting of the bordereau." When told that the letters were of a recent date and bore a Paris postmark, the expert had a ready answer. "It is obvious," he said, "that the Jews have been training someone to imitate Dreyfus's handwriting."

Bertillon's theory seemed too outlandish to Picquart to be credible and he took his discovery about the identical handwritings to General Boisdeffre. Distinctly discomfited, Boisdeffre tried to extricate himself from the matter by referring Picquart to General Charles Gonse, the Deputy Chief of the General Staff, to whom the Statistical Section was officially responsible. Gonse listened to Picquart, compared the photographs of the Esterhazy letters with the bordereau, shrugged and said, "Well, it looks as if a mistake has been made." When Picquart pressed him for suggestions on how to follow up on what had been learned, Gonse gave not a suggestion but an order. "Keep the Dreyfus and Esterhazy cases separate," he commanded. He reminded Picquart that the Dreyfus Case was closed and told him that because the bordereau was part of that closed case, it could not be used against Esterhazy. If the colonel wished to press charges against Esterhazy he would have to do so on the basis of the petit bleu in conjunction with other evidence which might be turned up in the future. Picquart hurried back to General Boisdeffre but he could not interest that officer in countermanding Gonse's order. "Wait for a while before you report all this to the War Minister," he advised.

Suddenly, Dreyfus's name was in the news again. Newspaper headlines screamed the report that he had escaped from Devil's Island; accompanying articles implied that the traitor's escape could be traced directly to laxity on the part of the Minister of Colonies. There was absolutely no substance to the report. It was, in fact, the result of a rumor that Mathieu Dreyfus had deliberately planted in the desperate hope that it would reawaken public interest in his brother's case. Had he guessed what dire side-effects the rumor would have, he would never have taken the step. An official cable of inquiry was quickly sent off to French Guiana and within twenty-four hours it was answered by the reassuring word that Dreyfus was still safely imprisoned but, by that time, the Minister of Colonies had been badly frightened by the rumor and its sensational repercussions in the press. He cabled instructions to Dreyfus's warders to build a double palisade around the prisoner's hut and to keep the prisoner in irons each night until the job was completed.

For forty-four nights Dreyfus's feet were shackled to the foot of his cot by iron bars in such a way that he was immobilized in one position until his guards saw fit to release him. He was not even informed of the reason for his torture until two days after it began when the commandant of the island came to see him and explained that the irons were not a punishment, but "a measure of precaution." How bitterly ironic that seemed to Dreyfus who was, as he wrote in his diary that day, "already watched like a wild beast night and day by a guard armed with a rifle and a revolver!" The commandant's heart was moved by the sight of his prisoner's torment and he registered an official protest against the orders he had received. His answer was a recall to France; he was replaced by a brutal prison official named Lebon who could be relied on to do his duty without being troubled by pangs of pity.

Now it seemed to Dreyfus that in spite of his firm resolve he could not possibly last much longer. While the palisades were being erected he was kept inside his hut at all times and, when they were finally completed and he was allowed to exercise outdoors again, he found that the new wooden walls deprived him of his only consolation, the sight of the sea. Vermin, spidercrabs and swarms of mosquitoes, these were his companions — these and the ever present, ever silent armed guards. His world was tightly bounded by the palisades; overhead the sun blazed mercilessly; intermittent bouts of fever robbed him of his strength and he was haunted by the fear of going mad. And yet, as he lay in his cot through the hot nights, his muddled thoughts turning round and round, time and again he thought he heard a voice speaking to him of Lucie and his children or, opening his eyes and looking up through the window of his hut to the sky, he thought he saw an eerie light that seemed to foretell the dawn of a new day for him. And then he would carefully repeat to himself the reasons he had for continuing to live: his honor must be restored, his children's name must be cleared — he must live lest his death cut off all efforts to run the real traitor to earth. Yes, he must live. He would write to Lucie and urge her again to press the search. Thus, Dreyfus painfully pulled himself out of the depths of despair and, in spite of everything, he lived.

Knowing nothing of his brother's new torments, Mathieu rejoiced when he saw the newspapers jump to the bait of his escape rumor. The blatantly anti-Semitic papers proclaimed that "the international Jewish Syndicate" was making plans to bribe Dreyfus's warders into letting him go but other newspapers evoked some sympathy for Dreyfus by feeding their sensation-hungry readers details about the prisoner's miserable existence on Devil's Island. And then, best of all, early in September, the newspaper, *L'Eclair*, printed an article implying that considerably more than handwriting analysis had been involved in Dreyfus's conviction. This was exactly the sort of speculation Mathieu had hoped to provoke.

Picquart interpreted the *Eclair* article as evidence that the Dreyfus family was making headway in its attempt to prove Alfred Dreyfus innocent. When, the next day, the Nationalist Deputy Castelin publicly announced his intention to question the government on its conduct of the Dreyfus Case as soon as Parliament reopened, Picquart was sure that the Army was in dire straits. Disregarding General Boisdeffre's advice, he went to the Minister of War, General Billot, and revealed to the general the discoveries he had made about Esterhazy. He urged Billot to expose Esterhazy, admit that the 1894 court-martial had made a gross error, and free Dreyfus before all these actions were forced on the War Office. Billot, however, refused to make a move.

On September 14, a second article in *L'Eclair* stated flatly that secret evidence had been used against Dreyfus in clear violation of the law. Now seriously worried, Picquart went back to General Gonse and begged him to act before the War Office found itself in an indefensible position. Gonse could not or would not see the urgency of the situation. "Why do you make such a point of getting Dreyfus off Devil's Island?" he asked Picquart. "But, General, he is innocent," Picquart replied. "That," said Gonse, "is not enough. You seem to forget, Colonel, that high ranking generals, Mercier to name one, are involved in this. No, the case is closed." Unable to believe what he had heard, Picquart cried out, "But, since he is innocent!" "That is unimportant," said Gonse, "that is not a consideration which should be brought into the reckoning." Desperate now, Picquart appealed to the general's self-interest; he reminded him that the Dreyfus family was working night and day to establish proof of Alfred

Dreyfus's innocence and might, at any moment, succeed. Gonse answered only, "If you say nothing, the facts will never be known."

Enraged and momentarily oblivious of differences in rank, Picquart turned on his heel and walked to the door. Pausing for a moment before leaving the room, he said coldly, "General, this is abominable. I will not carry this secret to my grave." Later, however, as his fury ebbed, Picquart realized that, for the time being at least, his hands were tied. He was, after all, a soldier and orders were orders; he could do nothing but bide his time and keep a careful eye on Esterhazy. Perhaps, if the blackguard were given enough rope, he would hang himself.

But Picquart reckoned without Major Henry. Reading the *Eclair* articles and hearing rumors that Picquart was on a crusade to clear Dreyfus's name and brand Esterhazy as the traitor, Henry was frightened — not for Esterhazy, but for himself. Picquart's charges certainly threatened his aristocratic friend, Esterhazy, but that, to Henry, was a minor matter. Of primary importance to him was the fact that his own career was endangered. Remembering how loudly and positively he had stated his conviction that Dreyfus was guilty at the 1894 court-martial, Henry decided that he could not afford to have the case reopened. If the evidence against Dreyfus was weak, then it must be made to appear stronger; if Picquart was a threat, then Picquart must be dealt with. With careful calculation, Henry mapped out a campaign of action and set to work.

During September and October of 1896, Henry "nourished" the Dreyfus file. First, he took from the Section's files an old plum from Madame Bastian's harvest, a draft of a note from von Schwartzkoppen to Panizzardi; and, erasing a P and writing a D in its place, he made the note read:

> Yesterday evening I had to send for the doctor who
> has forbidden me to go out. Since I cannot come to
> you, will you please come to me tomorrow morning
> for D. has brought me a number of interesting things
> and the work must be shared as we have only ten days
> left.

Next, with the aid of an expert forger employed by the
Statistical Section in its "document factory," Henry manu-
factured a note from the Italian attaché, Panizzardi, to his
German counterpart, using a text which he had made up out
of his head. This one, calculated to be definitely damning for
Dreyfus, read:

> I have read that a Deputy is going to ask about
> Dreyfus. If new explanations are required at Rome, I
> shall say I never had any relations with this Jew. You
> understand. If you are asked, say the same thing, for
> no one must ever know what happened to him.

In order to "authenticate" the handwriting of this note,
Henry had his forger fabricate another, also supposedly
from Panizzardi to von Schwartzkoppen, containing an in-
nocuous message and bearing an older date.

Henry presented the products of his labor to General
Gonse as "newly found proof of Dreyfus's guilt." He also took
the occasion to remark to Gonse that Lieutenant Colonel
Picquart seemed to be positively obsessed with the Dreyfus
matter and that, as a result, the regular work of the Statistical
Section was suffering. Gonse was delighted with Henry's
"documents" and took them to General Boisdeffre, who
accepted them without question as proof that the Army had,

after all, sent the right man to Devil's Island.

Then, early in December, the newspaper *Le Matin*, exploded a bombshell by printing a photograph of the bordereau. This top-secret document, considered far too "delicate" to be seen by anyone not officially connected with the 1894 court-martial, was now public property. How had it happened? At the time of the court-martial, several photographs of the bordereau had been given to handwriting experts for their examination. All of the experts had been directed to return the prints to the War Office after the trial, but whoever had been made responsible for checking on the number of prints returned had been careless; one of the experts had kept a print and, two years later, seeing in the renewed interest in the Dreyfus Case a chance to make some money, had taken it to the editor of *Le Matin*.

The *Matin* printing of the bordereau photograph made General Gonse uneasy. The Dreyfus Case was supposed to be securely closed and yet it seemed to him that everywhere he looked he saw a new and stronger attempt to revive interest in it. When Henry, recently promoted to Lieutenant Colonel, assured him that Picquart was behind the *Matin* scoop, the general came to a decision. He went to the Minister of War and told him flatly that the War Office was not big enough to hold both a Picquart and a Gonse, that one of them must go. Billot made the best of a difficult situation by agreeing to send Picquart on "a short tour of inspection of the eastern frontier."

Once Picquart was out of France it was not difficult for Gonse to make sure that he stayed away. His inspection of the eastern border completed, Picquart received orders to proceed to an inspection of the Italian frontier. From there he was sent to the French African colonies where, General

Gonse wrote to him, he was sorely needed to organize the colonial intelligence service. Wherever he went, Picquart received friendly letters from Gonse praising the work he had already done and expressing interest in the tasks he was about to assume. Gonse's letters fooled Picquart; the colonel had been in Africa a long time before he realized that he was, almost literally, in exile.

In the meantime, Lieutenant Colonel Hubert Henry sat at Picquart's desk. In Picquart's absence he had been made Chief of the Statistical Section. His fondest hopes realized, Henry intended to hang on to his new position of power and he foresaw little difficulty in doing so. Picquart would have to be kept in Africa, of course, but that could be easily managed. Care would have to be taken lest the placid surface of the Dreyfus Case be disturbed again but Henry was confident that the documents he had manufactured would be sufficient oil to pour on troubled waters.

In spite of all Henry's efforts, however, the waters of the Dreyfus Case would become more and more turbulent; one after another subsurface current would be set in motion and these, in time, would merge into a whirlpool — a maelstrom threatening to suck all of France down into disaster.

8

Auguste Scheurer-Kestner

"AUGUSTE, my friend, listen to me! You must let me come to see you at your office. I have startling news about the Dreyfus Case — news that I must tell you privately!" It was a July evening in 1897 and the guests at a dinner party in Paris had just risen from the table and separated — the ladies, rustling in their silk gowns, had retired to the drawing room to gossip and to chat about the latest fashions, and the gentlemen, puffing on their after-dinner cigars, had gone to the library for brandy and talk of politics. There, one of the guests, a lawyer named Louis Leblois, had drawn aside another, his old friend, Auguste Scheurer-Kestner, the Vice-President of the Senate, and had whispered his urgent plea. "Yes, yes, of course, Louis, come to me soon at my office." Leblois thanked the Senator and the two men joined a group engaged in heated discussion of the Radicals' proposal to impose an income tax.

Sinking into an easy chair, Scheurer-Kestner twirled his brandy glass between his hands and sighed. The eternal Dreyfus Case! No sooner was he able to put it out of his mind than somebody succeeded in putting it back again. First it was Mathieu Dreyfus. Early in 1895 Dreyfus had come to Scheurer-Kestner with his pitiful story of a dishonored family name, a suffering brother and his grieving wife and children. "And it is all a terrible mistake," Dreyfus had cried. "My brother is innocent. You must help me to obtain a review of his case!" Scheurer-Kestner had been impressed by Dreyfus's dignity and by his obvious sincerity but he had had to refuse him. The man had no proof of his brother's innocence — only suspicions that the court-martial proceedings had not been entirely proper and a steadfast belief that his brother would die before he would betray his country. Later, the brilliant young Jewish journalist, Reinach, had told Scheurer-Kestner that he had suspected from the beginning that there was something rotten about the Dreyfus Case. Prodded by Reinach, the Senator had made some inquiries but had learned nothing more than that the War Office did not look kindly on anyone prying into a case that it considered closed. His old friend from boyhood days, General Billot, the Minister of War, had tried to squelch his interest in Dreyfus. "I can assure you," Billot had said, "that we in the War Office now have even more conclusive proof of the man's guilt than we had at the time of his court-martial." At that point Scheurer-Kestner had let the matter drop. Now, here was Leblois bringing it up again. Well, he would listen to what Leblois had to say. Perhaps it would be no more than a rehash of the same doubts and suspicions he had heard before.

It was a great deal more than that. When, a few days later, Leblois came to Scheurer-Kestner's office, the Senator listened to his story with rising excitement. It seemed that Leblois had recently received a visit from a friend of his school days, Georges Picquart, now a lieutenant colonel in the Army and, officially, the Chief of the ultra-secret Statistical Section. This Picquart was in Paris on a short leave from what he bitterly referred to as his "exile in Africa" and he had come directly to Leblois in order to entrust him with a mission. The colonel had written a letter which he wished Leblois to deliver to the President of the Senate immediately upon hearing of his, Picquart's, death. Worried at hearing his friend speak of his own death as something that might occur at any moment, Leblois pressed Picquart to tell him what lay behind all the mystery and, finally, Picquart complied.

Leblois outlined to Scheurer-Kestner the story he had heard from Picquart: the colonel's discovery of proof that Dreyfus was, after all, innocent and an infantry captain named Walsin-Esterhazy was the actual author of the infamous bordereau; the response of Picquart's superiors to his findings — first, indifference and then, hostility; Picquart's agreement to remain silent about what he knew qualified by a vow to General Gonse that he would not carry his secret to his grave; his subsequent banishment on a series of inspection tours that culminated in what was clearly permanent duty in the African colonies. "But death, Georges, why do you speak of your death?" Leblois has asked Picquart and the colonel had answered that he had two reasons for his morbid preoccupation. First, a nasty fall from his horse had recently brought home to him how easily he could die with his secret untold — it was while he was still shaken by this experience that he had written the letter he was now placing in Leblois's hands; and second, he was convinced that he was regarded by the generals as such a threat to their security that they would not scruple to eliminate him by whatever means came to hand.

Profoundly disturbed by what he heard, Leblois had urged Picquart to allow him to spread the story where it would do the most good but, at first, Picquart would not hear of it. He was, he told Leblois, a soldier whose duty it was to obey

Hubert Henry after his promotion to Lieutenant Colonel

General Auguste Mercier, Minister of War at the time of Dreyfus's arrest

Captain Alfred Dreyfus, before his arrest

(*Culver Pictures, Inc.*)

Major Du Paty de Clam

General Raoul Boisdeffre, Chief of the General Staff

(*Culver Pictures, Inc.*)

Dreyfus's degradation

Devil's Island as it looked when Dreyfus was held prisoner there

(*Culver Pictures, Inc.*)

Auguste Scheurer-Kestner, Vice-President of the Senate

Major Count Ferdinand Walsin-Esterhazy

orders no matter how repugnant those orders might be. Though the thought of an innocent man suffering for another's crime tortured him, he could not bring himself to be disloyal to his superiors who had ordered him to be silent. Leblois argued with him, pointing out that he owed it not only to Dreyfus but to himself to let the truth be known; Dreyfus must be vindicated and he, Picquart, must be rescued from the injustice and danger of his present situation. At last, just before he was to return to Africa, Picquart relented. He gave Leblois permission to speak to a few influential people with the proviso that his, Picquart's, name be kept out of the matter until he consented to its use. He was adamant on one other point. Leblois must not confide his story to the Dreyfus family; in spite of his intense desire to see justice done, Picquart could not help considering an alliance with the generals' "adversary," the Dreyfus family, as the height of disloyalty to the Army.

Picquart had gone back to Africa and Leblois had come to Scheurer-Kestner. The Senator's reputation for integrity and dauntless courage had convinced him, Leblois told Scheurer-Kestner, that he, above all others, would spring to the defense of an unjustly convicted man. Scheurer-Kestner knew that Leblois was not flattering him. It was true that he had spent a large portion of his life fighting for justice. It was true that he prided himself on playing the game of politics and coming out of it with clean hands. He had been present at the birth of the Third Republic and, as the infant democracy grew, he had always kept himself ready to guard it against its enemies. He loved the Republic and all it stood for; he would, if necessary, lay down his life for it. Now, he reflected, it seemed that he was being asked to sacrifice not his life, but his political career. As a longtime politician,

Scheurer-Kestner knew how easily a public servant could fall from favor if he espoused an unpopular cause; he knew that, given the present situation in France, if fighting for that cause involved casting doubt on the justice of an Army court-martial, such a public servant could see his career come to an abrupt end. The French people were so besotted with love for their Army that they would certainly see any "insult" to its honor as an insult to their own.

Scheurer-Kestner was almost seventy years old. Contemplating his age and the battles that lay behind him, the Senator ruefully admitted to himself that he had looked forward to spending his declining years basking in the respect and admiration of his countrymen. But now, all at once, all that no longer seemed important. He was old, yes, but he was alive and in his heart he knew that he was still a fighter. Faced with the challenge Leblois offered him, the elderly Senator felt his blood stir within him. No, it was not too late. He would fight once more to defend the Republic.

Moved as he was by Dreyfus's plight, it was the thought of the Republic in danger that impelled Scheurer-Kestner to throw caution to the winds. Having heard Picquart's story, it was clear to him that the generals had successfully convinced themselves that it would be best not only for themselves but for France as well if the Dreyfus Case remained closed. He could see how their minds had worked: a reopening of the Dreyfus Case would destroy public confidence in the Army's justice and honor and would lead to a disastrous breakdown in public morale. Scheurer-Kestner thought otherwise. The laws of the Republic declared the rights of the individual to be paramount; he was certain that if those rights were ever subordinated to the rights of the nation as a whole, the Republic would founder and France would step backward more than a hundred years into the past. When Leblois left Scheurer-Kestner's office, he carried with him the Senator's assurance that he would dedicate himself to the struggle for Dreyfus's vindication.

Having promised Leblois that he would not use Picquart's name until the colonel gave permission to do so, there was little the elderly Senator could do. It would do no good to come out and accuse Esterhazy as the traitor if he could not back up his accusation with proof. The most he could do would be to confer confidentially with one or two influential men in the Senate and tell them that he knew for a certainty that Dreyfus was innocent and that the bordereau had been written by Esterhazy; perhaps, knowing their colleague's reputation for scrupulous honesty, they would believe him and agitate for a review of the Dreyfus Case. This Scheurer-Kestner did and got no more for his efforts than friendly warnings about the danger to a politician in meddling with a matter that nobody else wished to touch with a ten-foot pole.

Word that Scheurer-Kestner believed Dreyfus innocent reached the newspapers and the sensation-mongers blazoned the Senator's name in their headlines: SCHEURER-KESTNER DEFENDS TRAITOR. VICE-PRESIDENT OF THE SENATE TOOL OF JEWISH SYNDICATE. The editor of one anti-Republic, anti-Semitic Catholic paper thought that Scheurer-Kestner's religion had led him to the paths of evil; it was well known, his paper stated, that Protestants were semi-Jews. Another paper assured its readers that Scheurer-Kestner's object in working for Dreyfus's release was the destruction of the French Army.

That was it exactly, General Billot told Generals Boisdeffre and Gonse, the French Army itself was at stake. After all,

General Mercier had given his word that Dreyfus was guilty and he, Billot, resting his confidence in the file Major Henry had shown him, had done the same; a reopening of the Dreyfus Case would sap public confidence in the Army and must, therefore, be avoided at all costs. Of course there was the distressing business of Picquart and his insistence that Esterhazy was the traitor. But, even if Picquart was right, the blackguard Esterhazy could be carefully watched and kept from doing further harm and Dreyfus could be kept on Devil's Island. Was not the honor and prestige of the Army of infinitely greater importance than the freedom of a single individual, a Jew named Dreyfus?

But what was to be done about Scheurer-Kestner's whispering campaign? It was obvious that the Senator had somehow gotten wind of the similarity between Esterhazy's handwriting and that of the bordereau and, although Esterhazy's name had not yet appeared in the newspapers in connection with Scheurer-Kestner's campaign for a new trial, it might at any moment. What would Esterhazy do in such an eventuality? The man was ridiculously volatile and might react in any one of a hundred ways; he might take it into his head to flee France or, worse, to commit suicide. Either measure would be taken as a clear admission of guilt and would lead directly to a reopening of the Dreyfus Case. It was agreed that General Billot would ask his friend Scheurer-Kestner to hold off any further action on Dreyfus's behalf for a short time and General Gonse would use the respite to work on the problem of Esterhazy.

Major Du Paty had been out of contact with the Dreyfus matter since 1894 and now he was transferred to the Second Bureau to work with Major Henry. Henry and Gonse briefed him carefully: there was, they told him, a campaign afoot to foist a Jewish crime onto a Christian, to substitute Esterhazy for Dreyfus; admittedly, Esterhazy was an unsavory character but he was innocent of the crime attributed to him; nevertheless, unstable as he was, Esterhazy might do something drastic if he heard himself accused and thought himself friendless — commit suicide, for instance — which would be disastrous for all those involved in the 1894 court-martial — Du Paty included; therefore, Esterhazy must be warned and assured of support — discreetly, of course. The little major swallowed the whole story whole; the situation strongly appealed to his overdeveloped flair for the dramatic.

A message was dispatched to Esterhazy directing him to go at a certain hour to Montsouris Park where he would receive information that would be to his advantage. Arriving at the rendezvous, Esterhazy was approached by a man wearing a false beard (none other than Du Paty) who whispered to him that he must not allow himself to become upset no matter what he heard said about him, for he had powerful friends who could be counted on to protect him if he diligently followed their instructions.

From that time on, Colonel Henry and Major Du Paty allowed their fertile imaginations full sway. Not bothering to keep their superiors informed of what they were doing, they manipulated Esterhazy as they would a puppet on strings. Almost every day, Du Paty donned his false beard and met Esterhazy at a secret rendezvous in order to bring him up to date on the Henry–Du Paty plan of action and to give him his latest instructions: he was to write a letter to the Minister of War announcing that he had heard of a sinister campaign to slander the ancient Esterhazy name and demanding that the Minister act against the despicable people behind it; he was to write letters to the President of

France, Félix Faure, threatening blackmail of high government officials if he was not protected; he was to write to Picquart in Africa accusing the colonel of conspiring with the Jews against him. All this Esterhazy did, embroidering the letters with a few flamboyant touches of his own. In one letter to President Faure, Esterhazy said that if the President did not act to keep his name from being dragged in the mud, he would not hesitate to appeal to his "feudal chief," the German Kaiser, who was "the suzerain of the family of Esterhazy" and who:

> . . . is himself a soldier and will place a soldier's honor, even if he be an enemy, above the paltry and dubious intrigues of politicians. He will dare to speak openly and firmly in defense of the honor of ten generations of soldiers. It is for you, Monsieur, the President of the Republic, to judge whether you are to force me to carry the matter into this sphere. An Esterhazy fears no person and no thing — only God.

Newspaper reporters dogged Scheurer-Kestner's footsteps. Would the Senator tell them why he believed Dreyfus innocent? Who had supplied him with evidence? Who was the Senator planning to accuse as the real traitor? Scheurer-Kestner brushed them all away. Handicapped by his vow to Leblois, he could tell them nothing and, besides, he hated newspapermen. He considered them a scurvy lot who thought nothing of assassinating a man's character in their morning editions and bleeding him white in their evening headlines. He told them that he would have nothing to do with them and they, their craving for sensation unassuaged, hurried to the office of General Billot where they were warmly received and supplied with a tantalizing assortment of fresh hints about "new proofs" of Dreyfus's guilt which they were encouraged to throw into their pots of rumor-stews. In appreciation for favors received, Drumont's *La Libre Parole* screamed to the people of Paris that Scheurer-Kestner had sold his soul for Jewish money. The favor of the Comte de Rochefort, editor of another militantly anti-Republic, anti-Semitic paper, *L'Intransigeant*, was not so easily bought. He denounced Billot's handling of the Dreyfus matter as indecisive and lumped the general together with Scheurer-Kestner, Premier Méline and Reinach as "associates in crime." The rest of the yellow press followed Drumont's and Rochefort's lead and added embellishments of their own.

Scheurer-Kestner badgered Leblois for permission to use Picquart's name. Without it he could do nothing, he said, and act he must; doing nothing to save Dreyfus, he felt himself an accessory to the conspiracy to keep the unhappy man on Devil's Island. But Picquart had not spoken and Leblois refused to break his vow. Scheurer-Kestner went to the President of France, hoping that Faure would take his unsubstantiated word that the Dreyfus Case should be reviewed, but Faure, intimidated by Esterhazy's threatening letter, received the Senator coldly and refused to help him. Next, Scheurer-Kestner went to his friend Billot and begged for his assistance. Listening to Scheurer-Kestner, Billot feigned sympathy. He said that if the Senator would promise to do no more on Dreyfus's behalf for a period of two weeks, he would make a personal reinvestigation of the Dreyfus Case. Such a reinvestigation was the farthest thing from Billot's mind. He intended to use the two-week hiatus to build up the case for Esterhazy's innocence and Dreyfus's guilt.

And what of Mathieu and Lucie Dreyfus? They had been

completely unsuccessful in their search for "new facts" and they knew nothing of Picquart's suspicions of Esterhazy or of his communication of those suspicions to Senator Scheurer-Kestner. They did know, however, that the Senator was on their side. He had gotten in touch with them and told them that though he could give them no details of what he knew, he could assure them that he knew beyond a doubt not only that Alfred Dreyfus was innocent but also the identity of the man who had actually written the bordereau. He wanted them to know, he said, that he would work tirelessly to return the martyred Dreyfus to his family. Mathieu and Lucie were beside themselves with joy. At last a man of real importance and influence believed wholeheartedly in their cause. What a brave and noble man the Senator was to allow himself to be pilloried in the press for the sake of a man he didn't even know! Excitedly, Lucie wrote to her husband that no less a person than the Vice-President of the Senate had come to his defense but her letter was returned to her. She was informed by the Minister of Colonies that the transmission of information to the prisoner about efforts being made on his behalf was forbidden. Scheurer-Kestner, himself, appealed to the Minister, pointing out that if such knowledge could give a despairing man a straw to cling to, common humanity demanded that he be allowed to have it. But the Minister of Colonies could inflict mental as well as physical torture without blinking an eye. It was he who had ordered Dreyfus into leg irons; now he insisted that the prisoner must remain in the dark about any and all efforts to free him.

Lucie Dreyfus did manage, however, to let her husband know that there was new reason to hope. Keeping careful rein on her exuberance lest the Minister of Colonies find her letters unacceptable and withhold them, she wrote only a hint of it here and another there. Dreyfus's mail was painfully slow in reaching him and it was November before he could breathe the heady aroma of optimism given off by the letters Lucie had written in August and September. Then, tears of excitement welling up in his eyes, he read over and over again the cautious phrases that seemed to promise so much: " . . . we see the clear path opening out before us . . . I can only press upon you to have confidence, not to grieve anymore, to be very certain that we shall attain our end . . . I am happy that [my letters] will inspire you with renewed hope and with the strength to await your rehabilitation. I cannot say more . . ."

But in the early fall of 1897, the situation in France seemed to be in stalemate. Scheurer-Kestner, unable to admit his connection with Picquart, did not dare to weigh his own opinion that Esterhazy's handwriting proved him the author of the bordereau against the battery of handwriting experts the Army could call to say the bordereau was forged; Mathieu and Lucie Dreyfus, unaware of Picquart's very existence, cast about vainly for leads to a "new fact"; and in Africa, Picquart received orders from General Gonse to proceed to an area of Tunisia where violent skirmishes with the natives took an almost daily toll of French officers' lives.

Then, in November, the stalemate was broken. Mathieu Dreyfus had hundreds of facsimiles of the bordereau printed as handbills and distributed throughout Paris in the hopes that someone would recognize its handwriting. The device worked. A businessman who had had dealings with Esterhazy came to Mathieu and told him that the handwriting was that of a Major Walsin-Esterhazy. In a frenzy of excitement, Mathieu rushed to Scheurer-Kestner's home. Was

Esterhazy the name of the man the Senator knew to be the real traitor? Could the Senator break his vow of silence and tell Mathieu at least that? The Senator could and did. The two men embraced and then conferred on what steps to take next. Armed now with the businessman's impartial appraisal of the bordereau's handwriting, they felt that the time had come to make formal charges against Esterhazy.

On November 16, Mathieu wrote to General Billot:

> Sir:
>
> The only ground for the accusation made against my brother in 1894 is a letter, unsigned and undated, showing that confidential military documents had been delivered to an agent of a foreign power.
>
> I have the honor to inform you that the author of this document is Count Walsin-Esterhazy, Major in the Infantry . . .
>
> The writing of Major Esterhazy is identical with that of this document. It will be a simple matter for you, sir, to obtain this officer's handwriting . . .
>
> I cannot doubt, sir, that having been informed of the name of the perpetrator of the treasonable act for which my brother was sentenced, you will see that justice is done without delay . . .

And the next day Lucie wrote to her husband:

> . . . Hope on with all your strength! How can I tell you my faith in the outcome and yet stay within the limits permitted to me? It is difficult and I can only pledge you my word that within a time very, very near, your name shall be cleared. Ah! if I could speak to you openly and tell you all the shifting and unexpected scenes of this frightful drama!

Mathieu and Lucie sat back and waited in happy anticipation for the results of Mathieu's letter to Billot. They felt certain that now the true traitor would be branded and convicted and that then nothing would remain but to welcome their brother and husband back to his homeland and to the loving arms of his family.

Scheurer-Kestner hoped with all his heart that they were right but, in the days that followed, he feared more and more that they were not.

9

Buildup for a Whitewash

ALTHOUGH French law required that an investigation be made into Mathieu Dreyfus's charges, the generals who had conspired to avert a reopening of the Dreyfus Case were not worried. Esterhazy, carefully warned and coached by Henry and Du Paty, had reacted to Mathieu's accusation with a display of outraged indignation that had seemed quite natural and correct to the French public and had prejudiced the investigating officers in his favor. The inquiry was to be held under Army auspices and although the officer in charge, General Georges Pellieux, was not involved in the plot to protect Esterhazy, his uniform guaranteed his bias in favor of upholding the verdict of the 1894 court-martial. If the general needed help in conducting his investigation, it could be expected that he would turn to the Chief of the Statistical Section, Colonel Henry.

During the first days of the inquiry it seemed that the generals' optimism was thoroughly justified. General Pellieux informed Mathieu Dreyfus that the bordereau, already adjudged the work of Alfred Dreyfus, could not be used in any way to support charges against Esterhazy; when, under Pellieux's questioning, Scheurer-Kestner admitted that his own strong belief in Esterhazy's guilt rested on Leblois's story of what Picquart had told him, Picquart was called from Africa, treated coldly by the investigating officers and castigated for "having revealed Army secrets to the civilian Leblois."

While the investigation was in process, Esterhazy pranced up and down the stage the Paris press provided for him, expounding loudly and with great feeling on the subject of his wounded pride. For the benefit of the reporters who flocked to his door, he postured and raved and vowed vengeance on the man who had sought to smear his old and honored family name. He would, he told the newsmen, hunt Mathieu Dreyfus down and shoot him like a dog. Esterhazy's vast audience, the newspaper-reading Paris public, applauded the major's brave words but agreed among themselves that he would do well to stop short of murder and content himself with giving Dreyfus a sound thrashing.

Might not Esterhazy be guilty as charged? No, said Parisians, that was unthinkable. True, the major was notoriously undisciplined and, if the stories about the women in his life could be believed, he was more than a little indiscreet as well, but a traitor responsible for a terrible crime already acceptably attributed to a Jew? No. Considering Esterhazy's noble birth, Parisians excused the excesses of his past; considering the much touted dangers presented by the "Jewish Syndicate," they resolutely closed their eyes to the possibility that the Jew, Mathieu Dreyfus, might be speaking the truth.

Then, suddenly, it seemed that Esterhazy's house of cards must topple. A certain Madame de Boulancy, who claimed to have been on intimate terms with the major at one time and who now wished to do him harm, tried to do so by placing in Senator Scheurer-Kestner's hands a packet of letters which Esterhazy had written to her. Dated between 1881 and 1884, these missives expressed not only tender admiration for the person of Madame de Boulancy but also the most appalling sentiments concerning the writer's countrymen. Referring to French soldiers, one letter said:

> . . . These people aren't worth the cartridges it would take to kill them . . . and if one night I should be told that I, serving as a Captain of Uhlans (German cavalrymen) would die massacring the French I should be entirely happy . . .

and another read:

> . . . I would not harm a puppy, but I would kill 100,000 Frenchmen with pleasure . . . What sorry figures they would cut in the red sun of battle if Paris were taken by storm and left at the mercy of 100,000 drunken and plundering soldiers. This is the feast I dream of . . .

Scheurer-Kestner delivered the letters to General Pellieux and demanded that they be considered as evidence against Esterhazy.

Word that his letters were in the possession of the investigating officers leaked out to Esterhazy and sent him plummeting from his dizzy height of supreme self-confidence into a deep abyss of despair. Mournfully, he explained to Du Paty that the letters did not, of course, reflect his true feelings about his fellow Frenchmen — he had written them in a fit of spite against the French Army by which he felt himself to be both unappreciated and underpaid — but, now that they had left the privacy of Madame de Boulancy's boudoir, he was sure that they would be his undoing. He would flee while he could, he told Du Paty, or better, he would do away with himself. Knowing that either of these courses of action would make a reopening of the Dreyfus

Case inevitable, Du Paty told Esterhazy to pull himself together and pointed out to the distraught major that his escape route was clearly marked — he had only to brand the letters as forgeries.

"Forgeries!" cried Esterhazy when the newspaper, *Le Figaro,* printed copies of the de Boulancy letters. "Atrocious forgeries!" echoed the anti-Republic and anti-Semitic newspapers which would not deign to print the offensive letters for fear, they said, of misleading the public. "Possibly forgeries," concluded the Army's battery of handwriting experts.

At the end of November, the official inquiry delivered its verdict: Mathieu Dreyfus's charges against Esterhazy were "unproved." Mathieu and Lucie Dreyfus were hard put to conceal from each other the despair each felt. What could they possibly do now that all their painstaking efforts to revive interest in Alfred's case had come, finally, to nothing? They felt helpless in the face of the overwhelming forces arrayed against them.

But, as the Army prepared to slam the door once again on all talk of the prisoner on Devil's Island, Esterhazy made it clear that he would not be content to let well enough alone. Intoxicated by the unlimited assurances of support he had received from Du Paty, he declared himself "unsatisfied"; the verdict of "unproved" was not good enough — the charges must be disproved. His long mustache quivering with indignation, the major told reporters that he could never rest easy until the odious stain on his honor had been publicly washed away. He demanded a full court-martial trial! If he could not have it, he added, he would remove the blemish on his name by suing Mathieu Dreyfus for libel. Panic-stricken, the generals informed Esterhazy that he could have the court-martial he wanted; it would never do, they agreed, to let this matter fall into the hands of a civilian jury.

Their plans for quickly disposing of Mathieu Dreyfus's charges against Esterhazy gone frighteningly awry, the generals looked around for assistance in keeping the Dreyfus Case firmly closed and when it was offered they eagerly accepted it from whatever source it came. Clerical groups working to restore the Church's political power and factions plugging for a king or a dictator to replace the Republic held out helping hands and the generals took them heedless of the fact that by so doing they lent the Army's august support to anti-Semitism and the campaign to destroy the Republic. Each day Army-inspired newspapers, Monarchist and Bonapartist journals and the clerical press joined forces to hammer home the same basic themes: Esterhazy's innocence, the moral decadence of a government that allowed the honor of its Army to be impugned, the dangers presented by an evil Jewish Syndicate that, attacking Esterhazy, attacked France herself.

The clerical papers did not speak for all French Catholics; a number of liberal Catholics, clergy and laymen, openly opposed both their propagation of anti-Jewish hatred and their campaign to undermine the Republic. Nor could these papers claim to reflect the views of either the official French Church or the Vatican; indeed, the policy of the Vatican in regard to the French Republic contradicted the aims of those Catholic groups that aimed to restore the French Church to its former position of political power. Although Pope Leo XIII did not advocate a complete separation of French Church and State, he advised French Catholics to cooperate with the government of the Third Republic and, in 1892, he told a representative of the newspaper, *Le Petit Journal:*

> . . . The Republic is as legitimate a form of government
> as any other . . . The United States is a Republic and,
> in spite of the disadvantages which arise from an un-
> bridled liberty, she grows greater day by day, and the
> Catholic Church there has developed without any con-
> flict with the State. These two powers agree together
> very well, as they should agree everywhere, on condi-
> tion that neither interferes with the rights of the other.
> Liberty is the true basis and foundation of the relations
> between the civil authority and the religious con-
> science . . . What suits the United States has still more
> reason to suit Republican France.

Nevertheless, the French clerical press was enormously influential. Most French Catholics looked back on the close Church-State relations that prevailed in pre-Revolution France as a bastion of national security and the Catholic papers, cleverly exploiting this widespread nostalgia for a Catholic-dominated society, were eminently successful in spreading mistrust of the Republic and suspicion of all non-Catholics — especially, Jews. Moreover, as the Dreyfus Case came to absorb more and more of France's attention, there was a conspicuous lack of comment on it from both the French Church and the Vatican. Approached by a group of university professors who believed that the confusion surrounding Dreyfus's court-martial entitled him to a new trial whether he was guilty or innocent, Cardinal Richard, Archbishop of Paris, refused to sign their petition; he told them that the Dreyfus Case was a matter for the courts and that it would be unseemly for the Church to intervene in any way.

Neither the French Church nor the Vatican made any attempt to restrain either the clerical press's militant anti-Republicanism or its virulent anti-Semitism. Inevitably, a great many Frenchmen took their silence to mean, if not approval, at least consent.

And so it was that, virtually unopposed, the Army, the Catholic press and the advocates of an autocratic past, each group intent on its own purposes, entered into an unholy alliance under the covering banner of nationalism. The generals claimed that the Dreyfus Case must remain closed "for the sake of France"; the clerical press recommended the exclusion of Jews from the Army and the civil service "for the sake of France"; *La Libre Parole* demanded the defeat of Dreyfus's "Jewish-inspired" defenders "for the sake of France."

By the end of 1897, the Dreyfus Case, no longer the purely military matter the generals had hoped to keep it, had entered the political arena. Although the Deputies and Senators of the French Parliament had, as yet, no reason to doubt the good faith of the War Ministry's assertion that the right man had been sent to Devil's Island, the prospect of the approaching Esterhazy trial had made some Deputies uneasy. As Alfred Dreyfus walked round and round the confines of his prison yard, wondering if his countrymen had forgotten him, his name rang in the Chamber of Deputies. Answering repeated demands for an explanation of the connection between the Esterhazy and Dreyfus cases, the Premier, Félix Méline, told the Chamber: "There is no Dreyfus Case . . . an accusation of treason has been made against an Army officer [Esterhazy]; this particular question bears no relation to the other." But Méline's bald statement did not still the clamor. The Count de Mun, the leader of the Right and a vigorous proponent of a Church-influenced Republic, took the floor and declared that:

> We must reveal the facts about the mysterious and occult power, strong enough to throw suspicion on the commanders of the Army, on the men who have to lead the Army and direct the war when the hour strikes. Let us discover whether that power is great enough to subvert the entire country . . .

The Count affirmed that this vital matter stood above the normal struggle between government and opposition forces and said:

> . . . There are here today . . . only Frenchmen anxious to preserve that common domain of our unflagging hopes — the honor of the Army.

The Minister of War, General Billot, addressed the Chamber and underlined his strong belief in the justice of the 1894 court-martial verdict. "The case has been regularly tried," he said. "On my soul and conscience, as a soldier and the head of the Army, I hold that verdict truly delivered and Dreyfus guilty." Impressed, the Chamber passed a motion acknowledging that the Dreyfus Case was closed, paying tribute to the Army and expressing disapproval of the leaders of the "odious campaign to disturb the public conscience." Three days later the Senate did much the same thing when it passed a unanimous vote of confidence in the government's handling of the Dreyfus matter.

Now the popular press set to work to prepare the public for Esterhazy's trial. Fabricating sensational stories from the hints their reporters had been given at the War Ministry, newspaper editors assured their readers that the Syndicate's campaign of slander would be confounded when it was confronted with the Army's "overwhelming proofs" of Dreyfus's guilt. Each day rumor enlarged these "proofs" until they assumed awesome proportions. Rochefort of *L'Intransigeant* announced that the German Kaiser was involved in the Dreyfus Case; actually, the public was told, the bordereau was of minor importance — it was merely the matter on which Dreyfus happened to have been caught — the Army now had evidence that Dreyfus had been transmitting material of immeasurably greater importance to foreign agents over a period of years. Admitting the striking similarity between Esterhazy's handwriting and that of the bordereau, the nationalist newspapers offered a simple explanation: the Jewish Syndicate had taught Dreyfus to imitate the handwriting of an innocent Christian officer so that he could, if caught, shunt off his guilt to another.

Scheurer-Kestner walked alone through the halls of the Senate. His associates, seeing him approach, turned their eyes away. National elections were only a year away and reporters for the anti-Republic press were everywhere; a reporter seeing a respectable Senator in conversation with Scheurer-Kestner might draw an unwarranted conclusion. Only a very few Senators believed the anti-Semites' claim that their colleague had been "bought" by Jewish money but most of them did think that he had allowed a misguided sympathy for Mathieu and Lucie Dreyfus to make him their unwitting tool. All of them agreed that, as politicians, they couldn't be too careful of their reputations. When the Minister of Labor announced on the floor of the Chamber of Deputies that he had spoken to Scheurer-Kestner only for the purpose of asking him the name of a certain pastry shop, everybody laughed but, at the same time, everybody understood why the Minister had felt it necessary to make the announcement.

Principles and Realities

AT FIVE o'clock on the morning of January 10, 1898, a small group of men stood in front of the Military Court on the Rue Cherche-Midi. A cold wind was blowing and there was still no hint of day in the sky but, as they stood together with their backs to the wind, the men laughed and joked in cheerful camaraderie. Probably, one of them said, they had been foolish to get out of their warm beds quite so early but, on the other hand, one never knew. There was bound to be a big crowd and the courtroom was small. They, at least, would be sure to get in.

Before long the anticipated crowd began to line up behind the early-comers. On foot, on bicycles, by bus and in carriages, Parisians swarmed to the Rue Cherche-Midi. There were men in bowler hats and velvet-collared overcoats, fashionable ladies swathed in furs, shopkeepers who had closed their shops for the day and scores of ordinary citizens who had found themselves "indisposed" and unable to report for work that day. It seemed that every Parisian who could spare the time, or steal it, had come to the court-martial trial of Major Ferdinand Walsin-Esterhazy.

An air of eager anticipation hung over the throng of shivering people. It wasn't doubt about the outcome of the trial that had brought them out in the cold — everyone knew that Esterhazy would be acquitted — but, rather, an expectation of "exciting new developments" and a determination to be present at the dramatic moment when the wronged officer would receive his official vindication. During the weeks just past the anti-Republic, nationalist papers had ground out a steady stream of rumors and leaks from the "secret" proceedings of the Army Commission of Inquiry investigating Mathieu Dreyfus's charges that Esterhazy had written the bordereau. As a result, every Parisian knew that a bevy of handwriting experts were prepared to swear that the handwriting of the bordereau was not that of Major Esterhazy. Every Parisian had also heard that a mysterious "highly placed" Army officer would be exposed as the real source of the false charges against Esterhazy. Who could this officer be? Self-importantly, one man in the crowd announced to those around him that he had heard from a "thoroughly reliable source" that the officer in question was none other than the ex-head of the Statistical Section, a Colonel Picquart.

Picquart's name raced through the crowd. Yes, yes, Picquart would be the man to watch. What was to be made of the Boulancy letters, though? Obvious forgeries. But what lay behind the Army's announcement that the public would be barred from part of the court-martial proceedings? That was unfortunate, to be sure, but one must assume that the generals had their reasons for the ruling — sound reasons, of course, having to do with national security. Besides, the public had been assured of being readmitted to the courtroom before the final verdict was announced. Ah, that was all that really mattered. How moving it would be to watch the brave major as he heard the court officially clear his name!

Soon after daybreak the French flag, the tricolor, was

raised to the top of its pole in front of the courthouse. The crowd, bored with waiting and glad of a diversion, watched the flag's ascent. For a moment or two all eyes were fixed on the flag. What did these men and women see? Did they see more than a blue, white and red striped piece of cloth flapping in the winter wind?

When the tricolor was first raised above France in 1789 by the men of the Great Revolution, its message to the world was brave and clear: The old order is dead! France is a land ruled, no longer by the whim of a king, but by law! There was a thrilling universality about France's Revolution; its rallying cry, "Liberty, Equality, Fraternity," was directed not just to Frenchmen but to all men; the set of principles that was to form the backbone of the French Constitution was entitled, not "The Rights of Frenchmen," but "The Rights of Man." Fluttering at the head of Napoleon's legions as they marched throughout Europe, the tricolor was visual proof that long established tyranny could be overthrown, that the weight of feudal oppression could be lifted. Seeing the tricolor, the downtrodden peoples of Europe straightened their backs; seeing the tricolor, kings and tyrants shuddered.

And yet in France, the land of its birth, the Revolution was far from won. Republican government, sown in pain and overwhelming sacrifice, failed to take firm root in French soil. In 1804, flushed with military victories and confident of public support, Napoleon seized power and announced the end of the First Republic; he proclaimed the First Empire and crowned himself Emperor to the acclaim of the French masses. Then, eleven years later, when Napoleon's seemingly invincible armies were defeated by the English at Waterloo, counterrevolutionary forces swept Bourbon kings back to the empty French throne. The tricolor was hauled down and the ancient banner bearing the Bourbon fleur-de-lis, raised in its stead. Twenty-five years after the Great Revolution, it seemed that France had been reclaimed by the past.

But the anguished hope that moved the men of 1789 lived on in the hearts of their sons. Resurgences of the revolutionary spirit deposed the Bourbon King Charles in 1830 and, in 1848, exiled his successor, the "Bourgeois King," Louis Philippe of Orléans. The tricolor flew again; France was a Republic again; again the bonfires of revolt flared throughout Europe.

Nevertheless, within a short time, French rebellion against the autocracy of kings faded once more into willing acceptance of authoritarian rule. The Second Republic's first President, Louis Napoleon, seduced by the legendary glory of his name, proclaimed the Second Empire and, unprotesting, the people of France allowed him to name himself Emperor. In 1870, visions of enhanced French power led Louis Napoleon into war with Germany and, in 1871, to ignominious defeat at Sedan. From the ashes of his Second Empire there emerged France's Third Republic, a weak, patched-up thing, born of haste, compromise and fear. Exhausted by war and humiliated by defeat, the citizens of the new Republic devoted themselves to the goals of order, security and revenge.

In 1889 a movement to place a military dictator at the head of France almost succeeded in overthrowing the Third Republic. A well-planned coup d'état collapsed when, at the last minute, the proposed dictator, the popular Georges Boulanger, refused to play the role assigned him. Boulanger fled France and the Republic continued to rule the country.

But by that time a subtle change had been effected in the hearts of many Frenchmen. The broad and hopeful patriotism of the men of 1789 had been superseded by a narrow nationalism compounded of fear of the future and a romantic longing for the glory of France's past. The factions of discontent centered in Paris — Royalists, Bonapartists, ex-Boulangists, anti-Republic Church interests, anti-Semites — all urged their countrymen to work for the restoration of national dignity and honor by dedicating themselves to the ruling institutions of the ancient regime — the Army and the Church.

And so it was that by the time of the Dreyfus Case the people of France had come to see their Revolution as past history. The Revolution, they believed, had asked too much and promised too much. They saw its principles as a package of abstract ideas too visionary and too dangerous to apply to modern France. Having found democratic government weak and unstable, the French people yearned for a strong leader who would concern himself not with ideals but with the realities of protecting France from her enemies and restoring her to her former position of power.

Was there, then, no room left for the Republic in the hearts of Frenchmen? Now, in 1898, as the Esterhazy trial was about to open, was the tricolor no more than a piece of cloth flapping in the wind? Was France so disillusioned and afraid that a return to autocracy was inevitable? There were some Frenchmen who thought otherwise, men who could not see the achievements of the Revolution go by default. They, too, loved France but when they raised their eyes to the flag they saw neither the Army nor the Church nor the Kings; they saw the words "Liberty, Equality, Fraternity" emblazoned across the French skies;

they saw a nation proudly submitting itself to the rule of law.

Picquart was such a man. Reared in the discipline of un-questioning loyalty to the Army, he had found at last that he had to deny that loyalty for another, a higher loyalty to the idea of justice. Demange and Forzinetti were such men. Demange laid his cherished reputation on the line to defend a man he thought wrongly accused and then wept for a man he was certain had been unjustly convicted. Forzinetti re-peated his belief in Dreyfus's innocence again and again though he knew well that such blatant "disloyalty to the Army" would, as it finally did, cost him his position as com-mandant of the Cherche-Midi military prison. Scheurer-Kestner was such a man; as he plodded from office to office with his unwelcome story of justice miscarried, the aging Republican appeared to be willfully knocking down the sup-ports of popularity and goodwill on which his and all political careers balanced so precariously.

And in 1898 there were other such men. The journalist Georges Clemenceau was one of them. Clemenceau had been one of France's outstanding liberal politicians, the leader of the Radical party, until an unwarranted smear con-nected with the Panama Canal Scandal turned his party against him. Denied the forum of the Chamber of Deputies, he turned to the printed word to plead the cause of individual liberty; in articles published in newspapers and magazines, he called on Frenchmen to continue the work of the Revolu-tion, to resist Church pressure on the State, to take the edu-cation of their children out of the hands of the Church, and to recognize the insistent demands of the country's rising working class. (Although an outspoken "anti-clerical," Clemenceau was neither anti-religion nor anti-Catholic; like most French anti-clericals he opposed not Church or clergy but, instead, the attempt by some Catholic interests to extend the influence of the Church from the spiritual to the political realm.)

At the time of Dreyfus's arrest, Clemenceau was blindly biased in favor of the Army. He shared the intense desire of most of his countrymen for a quick revenge on Germany and, pinning his hopes on the Army, he gave its leaders unquestioning support. He not only applauded Dreyfus's conviction but also publicly announced his regret that Dreyfus's military judges had been precluded by law from passing the death sentence.

During the summer of 1897, however, Clemenceau heard that his old friend of thirty years' standing, Senator Scheurer-Kestner, was struggling to secure a new trial for Dreyfus. Knowing that the Senator was not a man to take up a cause lightly, he went to see him and questioned him about his knowledge of the Dreyfus Case. After listening to Scheurer-Kestner's story, Clemenceau came to the reluctant conclusion, not that Dreyfus was innocent — he couldn't yet bring himself to believe that the Army had sent the wrong man to Devil's Island — but that Dreyfus had been convicted in an illegal manner.

With his long brow, heavy eyebrows, big nose and bushy mustache, Clemenceau at fifty-six looked rather like a balding walrus but those who heard him speak or read what he wrote forgot his appearance. It was his character that counted most and it was his character that would, many years later, earn him the world-known nickname of "The Tiger." All his life Clemenceau was a fighter; he was uncommonly brave and he was stubborn. Now, in 1897, he resolved to throw his weight against those forces that would make France something less than the land of truth and

justice he passionately wanted her to be. In the November 1
issue of a new newspaper, *L'Aurore*, there appeared the first
of a long series of articles in which Clemenceau, the skillful
politician and dedicated son of the Great Revolution, called
out again and again for "revision" — a new trial for Alfred
Dreyfus.

At about the same time, the editor of the newspaper
Le Figaro invited France's leading novelist, Emile Zola, to
write articles about the Dreyfus Case for his paper. He
printed three of Zola's pieces and these raised such a storm
of adverse reaction that shortly after the third appeared the
owners of *Le Figaro* fired their editor and informed Zola
that his contributions were no longer welcome. Zola was not
unduly surprised. He was used to controversy. He had lived
with it for a long time.

Zola, like Clemenceau, was fifty-six years old at the time.
He had heavy shoulders and a broad chest but he stood
only five feet six inches tall. His forehead was high and what
hair he had was thinning; he wore a small, pointed beard
and he was so nearsighted that he squinted even while he
wore his pince-nez glasses. His appearance was not at all
impressive. Looking at him, it was hard to believe that a
great many of his countrymen thought him vile and his
works base.

As a very young man Zola had decided that writing would
be his lifework and at that time he set his sights on the twin
goals of literary realism and literary success. By the time he
was thirty-eight he had achieved both — to a highly excessive degree, many thought. First doing exhaustive research and then applying a "scientific" approach to his
writing, Zola exposed all the seamier sides of French society
to his readers and they, appalled by the degradation, spiritual

corruption, intrigue and lust that he set before them, cried out, "It isn't so — French men and women don't live like this!" The noted author Anatole France announced that Zola was guilty of the one sin that could not be forgiven — lack of taste — and one newspaper summed up the consensus of public opinion when it called Zola's books "a mass of filth which should be handled with forceps."

Nevertheless, the French reading public, impelled by curiosity, a taste for sensationalism and, in some cases, appreciation of literary talent, rushed out to buy each new Zola book as soon as it was announced. If it, like its predecessors, roused angry indignation, Zola cared not a whit. He thought he had a mission to tell the truth as he saw it and he would not be swerved from his course. Seeing his works runaway best sellers in France and widely read in every civilized country of the world, he basked in his fame and shrugged off his notoriety.

During the fall of 1894 Zola was in Rome working on research for a new book and he heard almost nothing of the furor surrounding Dreyfus's arrest and conviction. Back in France at the beginning of the new year, his attention was momentarily caught by the case when, lunching at the home of a friend, he heard a vivid eyewitness account of the indignities the unfortunate captain had suffered at his public degradation. Zola thought Dreyfus guilty of the crime for which he'd been convicted — he had no reason to think otherwise — but he was, nonetheless, revolted by the account he heard of the mob's brutal anti-Semitism. Did civilized people revel in a man's abject misery? How archaic such blind, biased fury seemed! How thoroughly un-French! But, after all, the matter was closed; Dreyfus was back in prison awaiting deportation and the mob had dispersed; there was nothing to be done about it. Zola's plans for his new book weighed heavily on his mind and after only a brief stay in Paris, he retired to his country home in Medan where he devoted himself to his writing and completely forgot about Alfred Dreyfus.

It wasn't until almost three years later that Zola began to learn the hidden truths of the Dreyfus Case. He came to Paris to spend the winter of 1897 and shortly after his arrival there he was introduced to Picquart's lawyer friend, Louis Leblois. The story that Leblois told him sent him to see Scheurer-Kestner. Deeply impressed by the Senator's selfless courage in pursuing a completely unpopular cause for the sake of a man he had never met, Zola carefully examined all the papers that Scheurer-Kestner gave him. He interviewed Mathieu and Lucie Dreyfus and when Lucie showed him some of the letters she had received from her husband, he was profoundly moved by the prisoner's anguished appeals for vindication. Sifting and fitting together the pieces of information he had collected and filling in gaps in the story with what he believed were logical guesses, Zola became convinced that Scheurer-Kestner was right, that Alfred Dreyfus actually was innocent of the crime for which he had been convicted. He was appalled by what he saw as a clear case of unscrupulous men taking advantage of their high positions to dupe a whole nation and to victimize a defenseless individual in order to protect themselves. Now completely absorbed, he determined to act against the evils he saw. As a literary man, he was fascinated by the "poignant drama" he saw unfolding and by its "cast of superb characters"; as a Frenchman who loved his country, he knew that he must abandon his role of recording the hypocrisy of society and, instead, walk onto the stage of life to combat

it. When the editor of *Le Figaro* invited him to write articles
about the case for his paper, he seized on the opportunity.

Zola's first article was a tribute to the courage and nobility
of Senator Scheurer-Kestner; the second, a penetrating analysis of the mythical "Jewish Syndicate"; the third, a blister-
ing attack on those public officials who clearly saw the
illegality of Dreyfus's conviction and yet, fearing for their
own positions, said nothing. Soon after the third article
appeared it became clear that Zola's messages were stronger
medicine than the French public wished to take. Cancella-
tions of subscriptions and angry letters of protest poured into
Le Figaro's offices and the paper's owners informed Zola
that from that time forward their columns would be closed
to him.

But Zola would not be stopped. Believing that truth was
on the march and determined to do everything he could to
clear its path, he turned to writing pamphlets which he
published at his own expense. He felt certain that if he
could just get through to the people and warn them of the
fraud that was being imposed on them, he could tear the
blinders from their eyes. Hoping to enlist the idealism and
patriotism of youth on the side of justice, he wrote *Lettre à
la Jeunesse* in which he called on France's young people to:

> . . . remember the sufferings your fathers endured,
> the terrible battles they had to fight in order to win
> the freedom you now enjoy . . . Thank your fathers
> and do not commit the crime of acclaiming lies, of
> fighting side by side with brutal force, fanatic intoler-
> ance and voracious ambition. If you do, dictatorship
> awaits you in the end . . . Who will, if you do not, at-
> tempt the sublime adventure, plunge headlong into
> a dangerous and superb cause, take a stand against

the people in the name of justice? . . . are you not
ashamed that the elders, the old ones, are the ones who
are reacting passionately, who are doing your job of
generous impulse?

Zola's books were best sellers; not so his pamphlets. Nevertheless, they had an effect — not on the young people from
whom Zola hoped for so much, but on some of France's
leading intellectuals. A group of university professors,
scientists, artists and literary men began to form around
Zola, Scheurer-Kestner and Clemenceau — among them the
authors Anatole France (who did not like Zola's literary
style but wholeheartedly approved his political ideals) and
Marcel Proust; the painter Claude Monet; the ex-Minister
of Justice, Ludovic Trarieux; and the noted professor of
chemistry at the Ecole Polytechnique, Edouard Grimaux.

In France, only Paris was aroused by the Dreyfus Case;
the provinces heard little about it and what they heard they
dismissed as "politics," a field of endeavor that most Frenchmen gladly left to the sophisticated Parisians, who appeared
to have the time for it. Outside of France, however, the
case was attracting more and more notice. The often-
repeated official German and Italian denials of any dealings
with Dreyfus, ignored in France, were generally believed
elsewhere. The names of Zola, Clemenceau and Scheurer-
Kestner had long been known and respected beyond the
boundaries of France and now their voices calling for justice
for Dreyfus seemed to be crying in a wilderness — a wilderness in which the power of a small military clique was
relentlessly dimming the passion for reason, truth and liberty
that had made France a symbol of enlightenment to the
world. From every direction came appeals to France to open
her eyes and see the danger. In the Paris press, however,

editorials denounced all "outside interference"; this was a French matter, the newspapers said, a matter only Frenchmen could understand.

Scheurer-Kestner, Zola, Clemenceau and the other advocates of a new trial were called "revisionists," "Dreyfusards" and "agents of the Jewish Syndicate" by those who opposed them; they, in turn, proudly announced that they were, in fact, a syndicate — not a Jewish syndicate but a syndicate of the truth. But at the end of 1897, the Dreyfusards were pitifully few in number; their voices were all but drowned out in the chorus of rancorous vilification that rose from the "nationalist" press — the Catholic and anti-Semitic newspapers and the journals that regularly reflected the Army point of view. According to these papers, shameful doubt had been cast on the quality of Army justice for the purpose of weakening the people's confidence in their military leaders — the Jews were to blame; an innocent Christian, a man of the highest honor, had been branded a traitor — the Jews were to blame; Dreyfusard agitation, diabolically planned and fomented, was sapping the nation's strength — the Jews were to blame. By the beginning of 1898 virulent anti-Semitism had spread like a black fog over all of France and as hate walked the streets of their city, Parisians, unmindful of danger, eagerly awaited the spectacle of Major Esterhazy's court-martial.

Now, on the morning of January 10, 1898, the patience of the crowd outside the courthouse on the Rue Cherche-Midi was finally rewarded. The doors of the courthouse were thrown open and, pushing and shoving, the eager throng surged forward and crowded into the courtroom.

The court-martial judges went through the motions of a

search for justice but it was obvious from the start that
the script for the trial and its ending had been written in
advance by the Army's Commission of Inquiry. Esterhazy
was questioned but when he tripped himself up with contradictory statements he was not pressed. Picquart, called from
Africa as a witness, was allowed to tell his story (he told only
part of it — still intent on protecting the Army he loved, he
steered clear of implicating his superiors in the conspiracy
against Dreyfus) and Scheurer-Kestner was permitted to state
his conviction that Dreyfus could not possibly have written
the bordereau, but the judges made it clear that they gave
little weight to Scheurer-Kestner's word and they treated
Picquart coldly.

On the second day of the trial, the testimony of the handwriting experts and that of Colonel Henry was taken behind
closed doors. As the newspapers had predicted they
would, the experts cleared Esterhazy of having written the
bordereau. On the witness stand, Colonel Henry calmly
stated that he had seen Picquart show his lawyer friend,
Leblois, confidential Army files at the offices of the Statistical
Section. When Picquart and Leblois vehemently denied
Henry's charge, the judges stared at them blankly.

After the last witness had been heard, the officer-judges
conferred — for five minutes. Then the courtroom doors
were opened and the public which had been waiting impatiently outside was invited in. The presiding judge
pounded his gavel for quiet and then announced the verdict:
the seven judges had voted unanimously for acquittal!
Esterhazy was immediately surrounded by a throng of joyful
men and women. Tears streaming from their eyes, they
pushed and shoved each other aside in their anxiety to
embrace their hero. Beaming, Esterhazy basked in their

acclaim. When at last a path to the door was cleared for him and he stepped outside onto the courthouse steps, the overflow crowd outside burst into a thunderous ovation. Long live Esterhazy! Long live the Army! Death to the Jews! Hoisted to the shoulders of avid admirers, Esterhazy rode triumphantly over the heads of the joyful crowd to his waiting carriage.

A CASE BECOMES AN AFFAIR

11

J'Accuse

As NEWS of Esterhazy's acquittal fanned out from the mob on the Rue Cherche-Midi, the people of Paris went wild with joy. Theirs was a fierce joy compounded of relief, self-righteous anger and blind hero-worship. With the Army's official announcement of Esterhazy's innocence all lingering doubts of Dreyfus's guilt melted away, love for Esterhazy as the symbol of the Army's honor mounted, and choking resentment against those who had dared to accuse him smothered all impulses toward reason and moderation. Everywhere in the city hysterical women clasped their small sons to their bosoms and assured them that they would one day be brave soldiers like Major Esterhazy. Strong men wept on hearing eyewitness accounts of the poignant vindication scene. As dusk fell, throngs of jubilant Parisians swarmed through the streets intent on giving vent to their glee and their hate.

On the Rue Bruxelles, Emile Zola looked up from the manuscript he was writing as hoarse shouts in the distance signaled the approach of another procession celebrating the day's events. Sighing in exasperation, he threw down his pen and pulled nervously at his beard. As the tumult in the street grew louder, Zola walked over to his window, drew back the curtain and looked down on the torchlit scene below. Vive Esterhazy! Down with the Jews! Chanting rhythmically, scores of exultant people were milling about beneath the window. When one of them, catching sight of Zola, shook his fist and screamed "Down with Zola!" the crowd broke into raucous laughter. Zola hurriedly stepped back from the window and the procession passed on. Flinging himself down at his desk and frowning in fierce concentration, Zola resumed writing.

He wrote most of that night and all of the next day. Once his valet interrupted him to bring him word that Colonel Picquart had just been arrested on charges of having communicated confidential Army information to Louis Leblois. On receiving the news Zola sat for a time with his head in his hands. Then he went back to work. He wrote, crossed out here and there, rewrote a paragraph and added another. He had his supper from a tray and then continued writing. Several hours later he was finished. Putting down his pen he reached for his hat and coat. He had decided that he would publish what he had written in the form of a pamphlet if he had to, but first he was going to make a try at getting it printed in a newspaper — he wanted as large an audience as he could get. Folding the pages he had written, he put them in his coat pocket, left his house and walked through the dark streets to the offices of *L'Aurore* on the Rue Montmartre. In the face of storms of public criticism *L'Aurore*'s publisher, Ernest Vaughan, had staunchly continued to print each of Clemenceau's revisionist articles; now Zola hoped that Vaughan would dare to print what he had written — his "Letter to the President of the Republic."

Although it was close to midnight, Zola found not only Vaughan but Clemenceau and several members of the paper's staff at the editorial offices when he arrived there. Asking them all to listen to something he had written, he waited until they had gathered in Vaughan's office and then read out loud to them the twenty pages he pulled from his pocket. When he had finished he peered anxiously at Vaughan. The publisher nodded. "We'll print it in the morning edition," he said. Beaming his approval, Clemenceau told Zola that he had a suggestion on how the letter could be improved. "The piece is good — very good," Clemenceau said, "but it needs a better title, something stronger. Why not use the two words you repeat again and again at the end of your letter — 'I Accuse'?" "Yes," Zola agreed. "You're right. It's a better title."

The next morning Parisians were startled to see the two words "J'ACCUSE . . !" spread in a stark black headline across the entire width of *L'Aurore*'s first page. Below, in slightly smaller letters, the words "Lettre au Président de la République par Emile Zola" topped six columns of small print. *L'Aurore*'s normal circulation was approximately 60,000 but Vaughan, certain that Zola's letter would attract wide attention, had worked his presses overtime. His foresight paid off; by nightfall 300,000 copies of the paper had been sold.

What was "J'Accuse"? It was the anguished cry of a man who saw the world he lived in turned upside down — crime enthroned and innocence condemned; evil acclaimed and good trampled in the mud. It was a distress signal warning the French people that they were being robbed of their most precious moral possessions while they slept. Seeing in Esterhazy's acquittal a ghastly perversion of justice, Zola had determined to tell France the truth and, addressing President Félix Faure, he had written: "It is to you, Mr. President, that I shall reveal this truth, with all the force of my revolt as an honest man . . . to whom . . . shall I denounce the malignant rabble of true culprits if not to you, the highest magistrate in the country . . . ?"

At the beginning of his letter, Zola had outlined what he knew of the background of the Dreyfus Case: the hasty, careless decision to accuse Dreyfus on the basis of inconclusive evidence; the play-acting confrontation scene staged by the "foggy" Major Du Paty; the subterfuges of General Boisdeffre "who seems to yield to his clerical passions" and of General Gonse "whose conscience adjusts itself readily to many things"; the dark cloud of tricks and expedients "as in some tale of the fifteenth century" which it was hoped would cover up an error that "at first involved nothing more than negligence and silliness"; the ridiculous secrecy with which the generals shrouded the Dreyfus matter — "a traitor might have opened the frontier to the enemy and led the German Emperor clear to the Notre Dame Cathedral and no more extreme measures would have been taken"; the General Staff's illegal "managing" of Dreyfus's court-martial.

Next, Zola sketched the events that followed: Picquart's discovery that Esterhazy's handwriting was the same as that of the bordereau, and his superiors' rejection of his findings. Referring to General Billot's entry into the case, Zola speculated that "there must have been, then, a psychological moment steeped in anguish" and he continued:

> . . . Observe that General Billot, new Minister of War, was as yet in no way compromised in the previous affair. His hands were clean; he could have established the truth. He dared not; . . . and so there was nothing but a moment of struggle between his conscience and what he felt to be the Army's interests. When that moment had passed it was already too late . . . Here it is a

year since Generals Billot, Boisdeffre and Gonse have known that Dreyfus is innocent and they keep the fearful thing to themselves! And those men sleep, and they have wives and children they love!

Zola's tone had grown more excited and angry as he wrote and, having traced the steps that led to Esterhazy's "arranged" acquittal, he burst out in indignation:

> . . . The war-office through every possible expedient, through campaigns in the press, through pressure, influence, has sought to screen Esterhazy, in order to demolish Dreyfus once more . . . what a nest of low intrigue, corruption and dissipation that sacred precinct has become . . . what abominable measures have been resorted to in this affair of folly and stupidity, smacking of low police practice, of unbridled nightmares, of Spanish inquisition — all for the sweet pleasure of a few uniformed . . . personages who grind their heel into the nation, who hurl back into its throat the cry for truth and justice, under the lying guise of "reasons of state" . . .
>
> It is a crime to misdirect public opinion and to pervert it until it becomes delirious. It is a crime to poison small and simple minds, to rouse the passions of intolerance and reaction through the medium of that miserable anti-semitism of which great and liberal France with her Rights of Man, will expire if she is not soon cured. It is a crime to exploit patriotism for motives of hatred and it is a crime, finally, to make of the sword the modern god when all human science is at work to bring about a future of truth and justice.

Finally, Zola had come to the meat of his letter:

> I ACCUSE COLONEL DU PATY DE CLAM of having been

the diabolical agent of the judicial error . . . and of having continued to defend his deadly work during the past three years through the most absurd and revolting machinations.

I ACCUSE GENERAL MERCIER of having made himself an accomplice in one of the greatest crimes of history, probably through weak-mindedness.

I ACCUSE GENERAL BILLOT of having had in his hands the decisive proofs of the innocence of Dreyfus and of having concealed them . . . out of political motives and to save the face of the General Staff.

I ACCUSE GENERAL BOISDEFFRE AND GENERAL GONSE of being accomplices in the same crime . . .

I ACCUSE GENERAL PELLIEUX . . . of having made a scoundrelly inquest, I mean an inquest of the most monstrous partiality . . .

I ACCUSE THE THREE HANDWRITING EXPERTS . . . of having made lying and fraudulent reports . . .

I ACCUSE THE WAR-OFFICE of having led a vile campaign in the press . . . in order to misdirect public opinion and cover up its sins.

I ACCUSE, LASTLY, THE FIRST COURT-MARTIAL of having violated all human right in condemning a prisoner on testimony kept secret from him, and

I ACCUSE THE SECOND COURT-MARTIAL of having covered up this illegality by order, committing in turn the judicial crime of acquitting a guilty man with full knowledge of his guilt.

In conclusion, Zola had announced:

I have one passion only, for light, in the name of humanity which has borne so much and has a right to happiness . . . Let them dare to carry me to the court

of appeals and let there be an inquest in the full light
of the day!
I am waiting.

"J'Accuse" was an act of courage. Driven by his rage
against the evils he saw menacing his country, Zola had
stepped out alone onto the field of battle to face a battery of
mighty adversaries — the generals, powerful and implacably
opposed to a review of military justice; the "patriotic" press,
irresponsible and outspoken ready to use fair means or foul
to destroy the revisionist movement; and, most dangerous
of all, the French people themselves — the people who,
suspicious and afraid, had identified their own honor with
that of their beloved Army — the people of France, one
minute gentle, reasonable individuals and the next, transformed by hate and fear, a swirling, torch-brandishing mob
capable of any and every crime. "J'Accuse" was an act of
courage and it was also an act of faith. Accusing, Zola proclaimed his faith in the France of reason and light, in a
nation that would, once her eyes had been opened to the
truth, rise up and fell the forces that threatened to sweep
her into the arms of autocracy. In publishing his blunt,
coldly explicit charges, Zola had risked losing everything he
held dear, even his life; he had done so in fear that if no one
spoke for justice, France herself would be lost.

Zola had need of all his courage and all his faith; "J'Accuse"
acted like a match set to a stick of dynamite and the reverber-
ations from the explosion it set off shook France to its
foundations. On the day it appeared, angry throngs converged on the Rue Bruxelles and when a force of gendarmes
kept them from storming Zola's house, they let loose a
barrage of stones and roared out their fury: Into the Seine!

Throw Zola into the Seine! In the days that followed, the
nationalist press fed public resentment with inflammatory
speculations linking Zola to the Italians, the Germans and
the "international Jewish Syndicate": Zola's grandfather had
been an Italian and Zola was, therefore, born to divided
loyalties; Zola's "disgusting" literary portrayals of immoral
and corrupt French people proved his devotion to Germany;
Zola had received bags of "Jewish gold" in payment for
writing "J'Accuse."

The mounting furor over "J'Accuse" spawned a strange
new kind of fraternity in the Paris slums. There bored,
restless young aristocrats in search of excitement came to
listen to the blandishments of anti-Semitic rabble-rousers
and to roam the streets in close fellowship with hoodlum sons
of the city's discontented poor. Spurred on by nationalist
agitators the ill-assorted youths raged through the city in
gangs shouting hymns of hate to the Jews and hanging
dummies of Zola and Clemenceau from scores of lampposts.

The hysteria in Paris spread to the provinces and from
there to the French colonies. In the pages of *La Libre Parole,
La Croix* and *L'Intransigeant* French farmers and small
landowners read thinly veiled invitations to vent their
righteous indignation on the sinister power behind Zola — the
Jews. Anti-Semitic rioting broke out in Nantes, Nancy,
Rennes, Bordeaux, Tournon and more than a dozen other
provincial cities and towns. In some towns having no Jewish
inhabitants, anti-Semitic demonstrations were staged by
people who had never seen a Jew. The worst rioting of all
erupted in the French colonial city of Algiers where agitator-
incited mobs swept down on the Jewish quarter in a four-
day orgy of pillage and destruction.

In France, fear spread over the land like a fog, choking

everyone, Jew and non-Jew alike. The average Frenchman saw a shadowy international combine plotting to take his job, his property, his country. If in his heart he harbored any suspicions that Zola might have spoken some truths, he was careful either to squelch them or to refrain from mentioning them in public; the newspapers had reporters (or spies, some called them) everywhere and a man who was so indiscreet as to venture the opinion that a new trial for Dreyfus would settle the whole hubbub, was more than likely to find his name listed as "a friend of the Jews" in the next edition of *La Libre Parole* or *L'Intransigeant*.

From the French Jews themselves, nothing at all was heard. Having seen the face of the mob, they were afraid. The ominous tinkle of purposefully shattered glass echoed and reechoed in their ears; the memory of flaming torches brandished in hate scorched their dreams. They told each other that they must wait and say nothing, that passions must be given a chance to cool off, that with the passage of time the people would forget their hate and the Jews would be able to live in peace again. Zola? Zola was a fool, the Jews said. They saw him trying to lop off the head of injustice with a single stroke and succeeding only in stirring up new storms of the anti-Semitism he deplored. And what about Alfred Dreyfus? Most French Jews believed that Dreyfus was innocent but they did not speak out in his defense. Afraid that anything they might say would only enrage the anti-Semites further, they held their tongues and tried to be as unobtrusive as possible.

But if Zola's "J'Accuse" was a galling irritant to cruel prejudices and a signal for brutal mob action, it was also something more. For a considerable number of Frenchmen it was a rallying cry and an inspiration. The poet, Octave

Mirbeau, thrilled by the shock of truth, wrote to Zola on the day that "J'Accuse" appeared:

> . . . I feel a violent desire to embrace and thank you because you have so magnificently illuminated what had been hidden somewhere in the dark of our souls . . . While you already belonged to posterity through your books, today you belong to history by virtue of the great deed you have accomplished for justice . . .

Even more carried away, the outstanding socialist, Charles Péguy, said:

> I do not know anything . . . that would resemble the rapturous beauty and power of this giant indictment, of this *J'Accuse,* which strings together line for line like a poem . . .

Clemenceau said in *L'Aurore:* "The cause of human justice admits of no compromise. You must be either for or against it" and, agreeing with him, more and more men found the courage to stand up and be counted for what they believed was right. The group around Zola, Clemenceau and Scheurer-Kestner grew larger and when a petition calling for revision was circulated, three thousand names were signed to it. Although every class of society was represented among the signatories, most of them were scientists, professors, artists and writers and, as a result, the word "intellectual" was promptly added to the yellow press's lexicon of smear words. Not all intellectuals, however, were brave. One, a prominent secondary school teacher in Paris, refused to sign the petition and explained to Clemenceau, "If I gave you my name, that ass Rambaud [Minister of Public Instruction] would send me to rot in the depths of Brittany."

What was the government going to do about Zola? Having slapped the French Army in the face was he going to be allowed to get away with it? No, he must be punished. Daily the clamor for reprisals against Zola grew louder and more insistent. Why did the government delay? At the end of his grossly impertinent "J'Accuse" Zola, himself, had announced that he was waiting to be prosecuted. Why didn't the government act?

The truth was that the government was afraid to take Zola up on his charges. The Prime Minister, Méline, was aware that there was carefully calculated method in Zola's apparent madness. It was evident to him that Zola wanted to be accused of libel and brought to trial for the purpose of forcing a reopening of the Dreyfus Case. Méline was extremely anxious to avoid such a review of military justice. Bowing to the pressure of the approaching national elections he had chosen what he thought was the safest course and had cast his lot with the Army; now he shivered at the thought of a public showdown in a civilian court on the propriety of the generals' conduct of the Dreyfus matter. Still, he told his War Minister, Billot, some official response would have to be made to Zola; in the Chamber of Deputies the government was under sharp attack from both the Right and the Left for letting Zola's accusations go unanswered.

While Méline consulted with the generals the nation waited breathlessly. Now the Dreyfus Case, a nagging inconvenience to a handful of Army officers, was no more. Confronting France in its place was the Dreyfus Affair, a tangle of political and moral questions that concerned every citizen. Must France, honoring her Army, turn her back on justice? Were the rights of a single individual of sufficient importance to warrant jeopardizing the faith of a whole people in its leaders? Where did the greater danger to France lie — in facing the demands of democracy or in denying them? Inspired anew by "J'Accuse," the revisionists begged their countrymen to rally to the time-honored cause of truth and justice while, in the opposing camp, the raucous patriots of the nationalist press pointed to "J'Accuse" as the epitome of Jewish-hired treachery. Outbursts of mob violence became commonplace and Parisians grew used to hearing the sudden clatter of horses' hoofs as detachments of cavalry galloped from one section of the city to another to maintain order.

Finally, in consultation with the Army, the government came to a compromise decision: Zola would be charged with libel but the charge would be confined to that small portion of "J'Accuse" in which he accused the second court-martial, the one that had acquitted Esterhazy, with having cleared a guilty man "by order." By so limiting the charge, Méline planned to confine Zola's defense to matters on which he could produce no real evidence and to prevent him from bringing any part of the Dreyfus Case into court. It was clear that Méline had hit on the best way out of a tight situation for both the Army and the government but Major Esterhazy didn't like the Premier's plan one bit. In the first place, having just had his name officially cleared by a military court-martial, he was extremely loath to expose it to the certainly less tender mercies of a civilian jury and, in the second place, he suspected that the generals, in their anxiety to save their own skins, would be quite willing to sacrifice his. He went to them and informed them that if, in the course of the Zola trial, he found himself in trouble, he would not hesitate to drag them all down with him to disaster. Blackmail is a very effective weapon when used against men in a precarious position. The generals hastened to assure Esterhazy that there were ways and means of arranging matters even before a civilian jury and they told him that he could count on their full support. On January 20, Zola and a sub-editor of *L'Aurore*, Perrenx, were officially charged with libel and their trial was set for February 7.

In the meantime, five thousand miles across the Atlantic, a lonely, tormented, fever-ridden man asked himself again and again what could have happened in France to explain a sudden tightening of security on his prison island. All at once, for no apparent reason, the number of Dreyfus's guards had been increased from ten to thirteen and a thirty-foot-high tower, topped by a gun covering the sea approaches to the island, had been built just outside his prison compound. What did it mean? Try as he might, Dreyfus could not think of a logical explanation. He knew nothing of Picquart's or of Scheurer-Kestner's interest in his case; he knew nothing of Emile Zola and he knew nothing of the mythical "Jewish Syndicate" which, reportedly angry at being foiled in its attempt to save Dreyfus by foisting his crime on Esterhazy, was now rumored to be plotting a daring rescue by sea.

12

Zola's Trial

ON THE morning of February 7, long before the hour
announced for the start of Zola's trial, hundreds of people
began to stream across the bridges leading to the Palace of
Justice, a massive hodgepodge of architectural styles stretch-
ing across the width of the Ile de la Cité, a large island in
the Seine. The people hurrying toward the Palace had no
hopes of seeing the trial — they knew that all the places in
the courtroom had been reserved for lawyers, newspapermen,
high-ranking Army officers and influential members of the
upper class — but they did hope to stake out advantageous
standing room in the Place Dauphine close to the Palace
steps. There they would be sure to catch glimpses of Zola,
Esterhazy, Picquart and various officers of the General Staff;
there, by clapping, whistling, hooting and jeering, they would
be able to register their opinions of each. Indeed, scores of
people in the crowd had been hired by anti-Semitic agitators
to do just that. In their case, however, their opinions had
been delivered to them, already formulated, along with their
five francs pay. Each hireling had been instructed to cheer
Esterhazy and every Army uniform he saw and to boo and
shout insults at Zola and his supporters.

As boisterous throngs poured into the Place Dauphine
the corridors inside the Palace filled up with people who had
been notified that they might be called as witnesses and

others who, though they had no real connection with the case, had gotten past the Palace guards by passing themselves off as stand-by witnesses. Waiting for the trial to begin, the corridor crowd divided itself into two groups, each claiming one side of the hallways. Ranged along one wall were those who wished Zola well; along the other, greatly outnumbering the Zola supporters, were the Army partisans. All at once, from the end of the corridor, a voice rang out: Here comes Esterhazy! and dozens of excited voices shouted Hooray! Vive Esterhazy! Gaunt and hollow-eyed, Esterhazy stalked down the hall, loudly acclaimed on one side and studiously ignored on the other. Another stir of excitement. Here comes Zola! Zola's friends sent up a cheer for him but it was lost in an uproar of clamorous jeers. Down with Zola! Death to the Jews! Throw Zola in the Seine!

Inside the courtroom the atmosphere was stifling. The stoves had overdone their job of heating the room while it was still empty and when the doors had been opened and hundreds of people holding special passes had pushed and shoved their way inside, the temperature had risen sharply. Every available seat had been taken within minutes and by the time court attendants succeeded in closing the doors, the crowd had spilled over onto the window sills and the steps of the platforms on which the judges and jury sat. Some audacious young men had even seated themselves on the floor along the walls.

The presiding justice, Judge Delegorgue, was fat and red-faced. Was it the excessive heat and the tumultuous babble of hundreds of voices in his courtroom that had sent the blood rushing to his head? Or, was it his consciousness of the heavy responsibility with which he had been charged

by the government? Delegorgue had been instructed to keep
the proceedings narrowly confined to Zola's accusations
against the Esterhazy court-martial and to allow the defense
absolutely no mention of the Dreyfus case during cross-
examination. Delegorgue thought that if he was careful he
would be able to carry out his instructions to the letter; he
had the necessary weapons at hand — his gavel and the
portentous phrase, "the question will not be put" (under
French law, a lawyer wishing to examine a witness, must put
his questions through the presiding judge who, if he deems
them proper, puts them to the witness. If, however, the
judge decides that a question is irrelevant or in any way
improper, he has only to say, "the question will not be put"
and the witness is thereupon effectively gagged). Nevertheless, Delegorgue knew that he would have to keep all his
wits about him when dealing with Zola's lawyer, the able
young Fernand Labori, a blond giant of a man with a
commanding courtroom presence and a courtroom voice so
thunderous that it was reputed to be powered by lungs of
steel. Labori knew all the ins and outs of the law and,
pursuing the interests of his client, he would certainly do his
utmost to inject the Dreyfus matter into the proceedings.
Delegorgue moved his gavel to a more readily accessible
position and looked out over his courtroom.

Most of the jurors sat gazing in frank awe at the spectacle
before them. They were all men of the middle class — small
shopkeepers, tradesmen and artisans — and they had never
before seen so many resplendently uniformed Army officers
or so many stylishly gotten up society ladies and gentlemen.
Some of the jurors stared at the principal defendant, Emile
Zola. They obviously found it difficult to identify this small,
bespectacled, mild-looking man with the ogre Drumont had

painted in such hideous colors in *La Libre Parole*. Under the jurors' scrutiny, Zola shifted uneasily in his chair. His forehead was creased in a worried frown and as he waited for the trial to begin he compulsively adjusted and readjusted his cream-colored vest.

Dressed in long black robes, the two defense attorneys stood behind their clients. Labori, tall, blond-bearded, broad-shouldered, was to defend Zola. Albert Clemenceau, balding and slanting-eyed like his brother, Georges, would represent *L'Aurore* and the paper's manager, Perrenx, who, though he was slated to play a very minor role in the trial, was technically Zola's co-defendant. Georges Clemenceau stood next to his brother. Although he was not a lawyer, he had applied for and received permission to assist Albert in pleading for the defense.

The din was deafening. Inside the courtroom the spectators chattered, laughed and called out to each other while from the hallways the loud voices of the corridor claque could be heard in heated discussion of the pros and cons of the case. At last Delegorgue beat a sharp tattoo with his gavel and called the court to order. Zola's trial was about to begin.

Zola called the opening shots. Seizing on his right to make an uninterrupted opening plea, he announced to the jury that not he, but France herself was on trial. In defending himself, he said, he would be defending France. He swore that Dreyfus was innocent. The fervor in his voice was striking but its effect was almost neutralized by a conspicuous lack of modesty in some of the words he spoke:

. . . By my forty years of work, by the respect earned

by the work of my life, I swear that Dreyfus is innocent. By all I have gained, by the name I have made
and my contribution to French literature, I swear that
Dreyfus is innocent. May all this perish, my work fail,
if Dreyfus is not innocent. He is innocent!

Dreyfus! The trial was only a few minutes old and already
Zola had succeeded in evoking the forbidden ghost, in
making the forbidden name ring in the tensely quiet courtroom. Delegorgue fingered his gavel impatiently as he waited
for Zola to conclude his opening speech. At last Zola sat down
and the examination of witnesses began.

Bang! "The question will not be put." Bang! "The question will not be put." Bang! "Witness, do not answer that
question." Again and again Delegorgue's gavel thumped.
Again and again Labori and the Clemenceau brothers were
frustrated in their attempts to draw useful testimony from
the witnesses they called. Although Delegorgue's repeated
exercise of his judicial prerogative was obviously favoring the
prosecution, Zola managed to restrain his impatience and
resentment until, on the second day of the trial, the judge's
gavel silenced Lucie Dreyfus. A murmer of sympathy had
swept through the audience as Lucie, veiled, dressed in
black, calm and dignified, had composed herself in the
witness chair. Zola knew that once she started to speak it
would be impossible for the jurors to doubt her honesty and
sincerity. But Delegorgue's gavel descended before she could
reply to Labori's first question. Blandly, the judge explained
that since Madame Dreyfus could not possibly have any
knowledge of the Esterhazy court-martial, no questions
could be put to her.

Outraged, Zola jumped to his feet and indignantly demanded "the right accorded to murderers and thieves, to call witnesses, to have them heard." When Delegorgue replied that in this case the law did not allow Madame Dreyfus to speak, Zola, furious and forgetting to measure his words, called out, "I do not know your law. I don't want to know it." Zola's bald statements threw the courtroom into an uproar. His earlier egotistical references to his own importance in French literature had irritated many who were already prejudiced against him when they entered the courtroom and now his impetuous outburst hardened many more hearts. Jeers and boos filled the air. In the midst of the confusion Zola tried vainly to explain: he was a good Frenchman and he respected the law, of course; he had meant to scorn only those hypocritical laws that stood in the path of justice. Nobody listened to him. The audience had already heard enough. How contemptible Zola was! What he had said was unforgivable! He was a wretch! A scum! Milling about wildly, the spectators banged on the floor with their canes and shouted, whistled and hooted their displeasure. Describing the scene for his paper, the reporter from the *Echo de Paris* wrote:

> . . . one sees peaceable, grave, decorated, intelligent, notable citizens, lifting their fists to this man and shouting with one voice, "Down with Zola."

When the court adjourned that day, the crowd in the corridor scrambled to get at Zola. When, closely surrounded by six of his friends, he managed to reach the top of the Palace steps, he faced a sea of howling hate-contorted faces. Pale and frightened, he hesitated. The mob started to climb the steps toward him. Labori, standing beside Zola, nodded to Georges Clemenceau and together the two men shoved

Zola into a nearby cloakroom and slammed the door. Outside on the Palace steps, a young Dreyfusard had the
temerity to shout Vive Zola! and was promptly beaten into
unconsciousness by the mob. Zola and his six-man escort
waited in the cloakroom until dusk had fallen and then tried
to make their escape through a side door. They found the
mob waiting for them. Screwing up their courage, the
seven men plunged into the throng of hostile people massed
on the Place Dauphine and fought their way to Zola's
waiting carriage. They made it just in time. As the door
closed behind them and the driver whipped up his horses,
the mob surged forward with the obvious intent of over-
turning the carriage.

The courtroom sessions that followed were exquisite
torture for the defense. One after another the Army officers
Labori and Albert Clemenceau most wanted to question
appeared in the witness box and, pleading "reasons of state,"
refused to answer the lawyers' questions. General Boisdeffre
made sweeping statements to the jury — the verdict of the
Esterhazy court-martial had been entirely proper and correct;
the War Office was now more certain than ever of Dreyfus's
guilt; Colonel Picquart had been suspected of working
against the Army's interest from the start — but the general
would not let the defense attorneys pin him down to
specific points. General Gonse played the same game of
evasion. Why, Labori asked, had General Gonse written
Colonel Picquart a series of friendly letters at a time when
the Colonel was already under suspicion? Gonse blandly
replied that since those letters were not relevant to the
matter under discussion, he would not respond to questions
about them.

General Mercier was the most tantalizing. The defense

was sure that it was under his orders that secret evidence had been shown to Dreyfus's judges and that it was he, therefore, more than any other, who was responsible for sending an innocent man to the living hell of Devil's Island, and yet not even their most skillfully phrased questions could elicit any meaningful response from him. Calmly, his heavily-lidded eyes cold and calculating, Mercier addressed the jury and explained his position: detailed references to confidential matters were out of the question and he must, therefore, confine himself to assuring the jurors that Dreyfus had been justly and legally sentenced. By now it was clear that a double standard applied in Delegorgue's courtroom. The judge had silenced Lucie Dreyfus immediately lest she refer to her husband's case; the generals, on the other hand, were allowed full rein in referring to Dreyfus and his court-martial.

When Du Paty was called to the stand a wave of chuckles rippled through the audience uniting amused Dreyfusards and anti-Dreyfusards in short-lived fellowship. Walking stiffly with the one-two step of a wind-up toy soldier and then snapping out an exaggerated military salute to the judges, Du Paty seemed to be acting out a parody of a correct Army officer. Once in the witness box, he explained at great length that his lips, too, were sealed — "reasons of state," of course. Du Paty meant to be impressive; he succeeded only in being funny.

On the fifth day of the trial Colonel Picquart took the stand and a sudden hush fell over the courtroom. It had been widely rumored that Picquart would be a key witness; Zola and the generals knew that his testimony could swing the balance of the trial either way. How much would he tell?

Ah, that was the question. Zola leaned forward anxiously. The generals fidgeted in their seats.

An invisible sword hung over Picquart's head. Ever since Esterhazy's court-martial he had been imprisoned in the military fortress of Mont-Valérien on charges of having revealed confidential military papers to Louis Leblois. A military Court of Inquiry headed by an intimate friend of General Mercier had recommended that he be discharged from the service but the War Minister, General Billot, had delayed accepting the court's recommendation. The implications of Billot's delay were plain: if Picquart would support the Army's position at Zola's trial, Billot would find it possible to forgive and forget; if, on the other hand, his testimony turned out to be unacceptable to the generals, his army career would be over.

Now, standing erect and proud in the witness box, Picquart began to speak and, before many minutes had passed, it was clear that in this man was the stuff of which heroes are made. Looking straight at the jurors, the handsome colonel told of how he had first become convinced that Esterhazy, not Dreyfus, was the traitor the War Office was seeking. Fully aware that what he was saying would cost him the right to wear the uniform he loved, Picquart described his shock at discovering that the secret Dreyfus file held no genuine proofs of Dreyfus's guilt and then explained how the arrival of the petit bleu in the Statistical Section had led him to connect Esterhazy with the bordereau. But Picquart was a tragic hero. Heedless of his own interests, he could not bring himself to tell the whole truth and thereby implicate his superiors in a miscarriage of justice. He said nothing of his arguments with the generals about Esterhazy and he did not mention the hypocritically friendly letters Gonse had sent to him in Africa.

Colonel Henry swaggered on the witness stand. Emboldened by Zola's failure to guess his part in the affair, he told brazen lies with cocky self-assurance. He said that he had seen Picquart show Leblois the secret Dreyfus file one day when Leblois was visiting Picquart at the Statistical Section. Yes, he could swear it was the Dreyfus file he had seen on the table between Picquart and Leblois — he had seen the "Scoundrel D." letter sticking out of it. Enraged by Henry's blatant falsehoods, Picquart jumped to his feet and shouted a firm denial. Henry's reply was, "Picquart lies."

In the meantime war raged in the Paris press. Pro-Zola journals printed the texts of letters and documents that Delegorgue would not allow Zola's defense to present as evidence and the anti-revision nationalist press countered by heaping insults and smearing insinuations on Zola, Labori, Picquart and Scheurer-Kestner. Some of the anti-Semitic papers went even further. They gave heavy-handed hints to Zola's jury on where their best interests lay by printing all their names and addresses in big black letters each day together with advice to readers to withhold their trade from men who succumbed to Jewish bribes.

Paris fell sick with suspense and each day the symptoms of the city's illness grew more alarming. Fistfights and brawls broke out again and again in the Place Dauphine and at night mysterious pistol shots were heard in the dark streets around the Palace of Justice. Newsboys hawking Dreyfusard newspapers were set upon by anti-Semitic hoodlums and their newspapers were snatched from them and set ablaze. Unable to cope with the continuing outbursts of violence, the city police repeatedly called on the military garrison for assistance and foreign correspondents reported to their papers that Paris had taken on the appearance of an armed camp. The tourist trade fell off abruptly and general business conditions worsened steadily as foreign businessmen, fearing that the turmoil in Paris might interfere with the fulfillment of their French orders, found new sources of supply.

Ten days after the start of the trial, tension in the city had reached a fever pitch but in the courtroom it seemed that the trial itself had bogged down in a quagmire of conflicting testimony. A defense witness swore to the truth of what he was saying; a prosecution witness swore that the opposite was true. Labori parried a government attack on Zola; the prosecuting attorney struck back. Where was the truth? Buried. Buried deeper each day under a thickening layer of pride, ambition, fear and prejudice.

On February 17, however, General Pellieux unwittingly brought matters to a head. Pellieux, the officer who had headed the Army's inquiry into Mathieu Dreyfus's charges against Esterhazy, was as anxious as Billot, Boisdeffre and Gonse to have Zola declared guilty. His motives, however, were quite different than theirs. Having come into the case late and having heard only the Army side of it, he was honestly convinced that Esterhazy was completely innocent, that Dreyfus was guilty as charged and that, therefore, everything Zola had said in "J'Accuse" was false. He had seen Colonel Henry's "proofs" of Dreyfus's guilt and it hadn't occurred to him to doubt their authenticity; neither Billot, nor Boisdeffre, nor Gonse had seen fit to tell him all they knew. Now, growing impatient with the endless round of charge and countercharge, accusation and denial, Pellieux cast about for a way of ending the whole distasteful Dreyfus matter once and for all. Unable to understand why the other generals had not brought up their big guns, their "overwhelming proof" that Dreyfus actually was the traitor, he determined to do so himself. Taking the stand, he told the jury of a letter "from one foreign military attaché to another" which the War Office had "found" in its files in 1896. Thereupon, he quoted from memory the text of the letter which Henry had told his superiors had been written by Panizzardi to von Schwartzkoppen but which actually had been composed by Henry himself to read:

> . . . I have read that a Deputy is going to ask about Dreyfus. If new explanations are required at Rome, I shall say I never had any relations with this Jew. You understand. If you are asked, say the same thing, for no one must ever know what happened to him.

Henry's florid face turned pale. The Generals Billot and Gonse (Boisdeffre was not in the courtroom that day) struggled to maintain their composure. They did not know for an absolute fact that the document Pellieux had quoted was a forgery but, not being fools, they suspected as much. By unspoken agreement with Henry they had kept it under wraps, using it only as something to be referred to vaguely whenever an extraordinary need arose, and at all times sheltering it under the covering shadow of "reasons of state." Now Pellieux with his blustering good faith had hauled it into the bright glare of the courtroom. Pellieux had blundered badly but the thing was done. Billot and Gonse knew that they had no choice but to close ranks and support Pellieux, to swear, for the sake of the Army and their own skins, that what was almost certainly false was true.

Gonse rose and, under oath, backed up all that Pellieux had said. Labori, however, was quick to point out that the "conclusive document" to which Pellieux had referred could not be legally considered proof of anything until it was produced in court. Insulted, Pellieux replied that since he had seen the letter with his own eyes, his word should be sufficient. Labori firmly said that it was not. Thereupon, Pellieux demanded that the Chief of the General Staff, General Boisdeffre, be called to support him and when Delegorgue assured him that Boisdeffre would be questioned the next day, Pellieux, completely forgetting that he was in a civilian courtroom, turned to an adjutant and barked, "Get a carriage and fetch Boisdeffre at once!" The uproar of shouts and cheers that greeted Pellieux's brusque command frightened Delegorgue into asserting his authority and, risking Pellieux's displeasure, he banged his gavel and adjourned the proceedings for the day. Throngs of overwrought men and women milled around the principals in the case, cheering the generals and hissing the Dreyfusards. Louis Leblois, unable to get away in time, was set upon and mauled by angry spectators and once again Zola was forced to leave by a side door.

The next morning General Boisdeffre took the stand, swore to the authenticity of the document in question, and assured the jury that if the letter were removed from the safety of the War Office files and the identity of its author and addressee made public, catastrophic war with Germany would be the almost inevitable result. Then, turning to the jury, Boisdeffre sternly reminded them that their final verdict would represent the will of the entire French nation. Speaking slowly, coldly and precisely, he added:

> . . . If the nation has no confidence in its Army's
> leaders, in those responsible for the national defense,
> they are ready to leave the heavy task to others. You
> have only to speak. I will say nothing more.

Twelve pairs of ears heard the threat. Twelve brains
registered its implications. Twelve men trembled at the
thought of what would befall them if they were to return
a verdict for acquittal. The General Staff would resign and
they, the jurors, would be held responsible for throwing the
country into confusion and leaving France to the mercy of
her enemies. In the brief silence that fell over the courtroom
as General Boisdeffre left the witness box, the clamor of the
impatient throngs outside the Palace could be heard. The
jurors had every reason to believe that the mob would seek
reprisals against men who had robbed the Army of its leaders.
True, they could be sure of a police escort to their homes
but once there what safety would they find? Thanks to the
anti-Semitic press all Paris knew where each of the jurors
lived and the way in which each earned his living. The
twelve men shifted uneasily in their chairs. It was clear that
each wished he were any place on earth but in the jury box
at Zola's trial.

Later that day Picquart firmly asserted his opinion that
Pellieux's "absolute proof" was a forgery. Surely it was not
just coincidence, he said, that this document was "found" so
conveniently at precisely the time in 1896 when the government was facing embarrassing questions about the Dreyfus
Case in the Chamber of Deputies. Besides, he added, the
crude language used in the so-called document was a dead
giveaway; it was highly improbable that one foreign military

attaché writing to another would choose such blunt words. Did Picquart's arguments seem logical and reasonable to the jury? Perhaps. But Boisdeffre's threat still rang in their ears and now as the trial was drawing to a close and the time for delivering a verdict approached, reason and logic weighed less and less with the twelve worried men, and prudence and caution loomed larger and larger as prime considerations.

At last all the witnesses had been heard and on February 21, two weeks after the start of the trial, the final speeches began. The prosecuting attorney told the jury that since the defense had not been able to prove that the Esterhazy jury had acquitted "by order," Zola must be found guilty of insulting the Army. In their turn, the defense insisted that, far from insulting the Army, Zola had valiantly tried to defend it. Labori pointed out to the jurors that it should be possible for France to honor her Army and at the same time refuse to allow a handful of military leaders to do whatever they pleased. In a voice quivering with emotion, Georges Clemenceau tried to drive the point home:

> . . . if the civilian society in its anxiety over national defense fell into the slavery of the military, then the soil perhaps could be defended, but morally the nation would be lost. By forfeiting the principles of justice and liberty we would give up what, to the entire world, has been the glory and honor of France . . . Free of racial and religious prejudice, you (the jury) will render inestimable service to France if you suppress the beginnings of a religious war that threatens to dishonor our country . . . Gentlemen, we represent the law, tolerance, the traditions of the French spirit . . . We appear before you and you will appear before history.

But eloquence was not enough and appeals to reason were not enough. The twelve men on the jury represented France and France had indentured herself to fear. Once again the jurymen heard Boisdeffre's warning: "The Army's leaders are ready to leave the heavy task to others. You have only to speak." Clemenceau had just said to them, "You will appear before history . . ." but the jurors knew that first they must appear before the throngs of angry people waiting outside on the Place Dauphine. Could they take it upon themselves to deprive their countrymen of the military leaders on whom they had pinned all their hopes and affection? Could they face the blood-lust of an enraged mob? It took the jury just thirty-five minutes to decide that they could not do either. The foreman of the jury announced the verdict: Zola and Perrenx were guilty; Zola was sentenced to a year in prison and Perrenx to four months; each was fined 3000 francs. The audience broke into jubilant cheers. Zola had only one word to say: "Cannibals!"

Paris celebrated the verdict in a frenzy of joy. Because one of Zola's wicked accusations had been officially declared baseless, Frenchmen concluded that they could forget it and all the others as well. The generals, their honor unblemished, had come out on top. Black had emerged conveniently black, and white, spotlessly white. The Army had been saved. France had been saved. Strangers embraced in the streets. Military clubs ran up victory flags. The city of Paris luxuriated in an overwhelming sense of relief and vindicated righteousness.

The crisis, it was officially announced, was past but, according to Méline, the Premier, its instigators would have to suffer for a long time. Speaking in the Chamber of Deputies, Méline said:

. . . The Jews who foolishly unloosed this prepared campaign of hatred, brought down upon themselves a century of intolerance — the Jews and that intellectual élite which seems to enjoy poisoning the atmosphere and inciting bloody hatred.

Implying that an excess of civil liberties lay at the root of France's recent troubles, Méline told the Deputies that the full rigor of the law would be applied against any who stubbornly insisted on continuing the struggle and he added, "If the powers we now possess are not adequate, we shall ask you for new ones."

Clemenceau was not scared off. Long since convinced that the Army had not only convicted Dreyfus illegally but had done so in full knowledge of its crime, he plunged back into the battle by publishing his own views of the Zola verdict in *L'Aurore:* General Boisdeffre, Clemenceau said, had placed his sword on the Code of Law and the jury had not dared to remove it. Not distinguishing between the official French Church and the Catholic press that claimed to represent it, Clemenceau accused the Church of deliberately fomenting anti-Semitism in order to cover up its vicious attacks on the spirit of the Revolution. He saw in Zola's conviction a triumph for an unholy alliance of Church and Army that had sunk France deeper into the criminal folly of religious and racial hatreds. A few brave Catholic priests published their strong disapproval of the fanatical anti-Semitism in the Catholic press but the official French Church and the Vatican remained silent.

Clemenceau's countrymen shrugged off his dire predictions of impending doom, but outside France's borders world opinion echoed his sentiments and foreign newspapers vied with each other in praise of Zola's heroic stand for justice. The London *Daily Graphic* said that the Zola verdict "reveals to us France delirious with anti-social passion . . . deprived of all the guarantees of an equitable administration of justice, and dominated by a military caste which openly mocks at the law. It is an ominous picture." The Swiss *Genèvois* said:

> . . . this sentence was passed under the insolently brutal pressure of the chiefs of the army, who have assumed the right to violate the law and to crush constitutional rights under their spurred heels . . . Poor France, what a retrogression!

Verhaeren, the poet, wrote:

> In this Dreyfus Affair . . . the whole of Europe has defended the spirit of France against France herself. The idea that justice should dominate racial and religious conflicts was implanted in the mind of the world by the Revolution. Mankind has become the greater for it; its gratitude was poured out on the people who had announced and expounded it.
>
> But it has come to pass that this same people has violated its own teaching as one might violate an oath. The world has not yet recovered from its surprise; protest is, and should be, universal.

The *Times* of London wrote that:

> M. Zola's real offense is that he has dared to stand up for truth and civil liberty at a moment when many saw the peril but no other was ready to brave the extremity of personal danger in order to aid in averting it. For that courageous vindication of elementary civil rights he will be honored wherever men have free souls.

The Italian *Tribuna* hoped that Zola would find consolation in "the unanimous cry of protest raised by all civilized peoples against the judicial crime committed in France" and the *New York Daily Tribune* summed up the situation by saying:

> M. Zola has fought a brave fight for the vindication of Captain Dreyfus. There is now need for a champion to fight for the vindication of France.

World Protestant and Jewish opinion was unanimous — France had allowed herself to slip backward into barbarism — and large segments of Catholic opinion outside of France came out in favor of a new Dreyfus trial.

Inside France the stinging barrage of foreign criticism served only to solidify public support of the Army. As resentment of outside interference mounted, Frenchmen became increasingly receptive to the propaganda of their own nationalist and anti-Semitic press: England, Germany, Italy, the Jews, the Protestants — all enemies! The French Army above everything! The Army is France!

To make doubly sure that Zola's conviction had written the end of the Dreyfus Affair, Méline and the generals moved to punish and silence Zola's principal supporters. Picquart was released from prison and then summarily dismissed from the Army; Leblois was discharged from his position as Deputy Mayor of Paris's Seventh Arondissement and Professor Grimaux paid for his stand at Zola's side by the loss of his chairs at the Ecole Polytechnique and the Agricultural Institute. There was no need to act against Scheurer-Kestner; during Zola's trial an election had been held in the Senate and Scheurer-Kestner had been defeated in his bid for re-election to his long-held post of President of that body.

But the curtain that the Zola jury had rung down on the Dreyfus drama was not the final curtain. It signaled no more than an intermission, a lull during which the audience would assess what they had seen and the actors would take up new positions. During the summer of 1898 the curtain rose again and an important new character, General Godefroy Cavaignac, moved to the center of the stage.

13

The Cracks Widen

It was a hot July day and all the windows of the Chamber of Deputies had been thrown wide open. In the back of the huge room small knots of excited Deputies were engaged in heated discussion. Fists were pounded into palms of hands, fingers were pointed, voices were raised and blood pressures rose with them. More Deputies entered the Chamber and while some joined the discussion groups others took their seats and busied themselves with shuffling papers. Before long the Chamber was filled. Hundreds of heads turned expectantly toward the door. The Deputies were waiting for the new Minister of War, General Godefroy Cavaignac who, it had been announced, would deliver a major address on the Dreyfus Case. Some of the Deputies had heard that Cavaignac would do more than that, that he would actually produce some of the ultra-secret Dreyfus documents that his predecessor, Billot, had kept so carefully under wraps.

What had happened since February? Why, five months after the Zola jury had "extinguished the flames of the Dreyfus Case," was the new Minister of War about to rake over old coals?

The truth of the matter was that in spite of all the government's best efforts the embers of the Dreyfus Affair had simply refused to die. Although Zola had been convicted of libel, the testimony at his trial and the revelations made by Dreyfusard newspapers during the trial had opened many French eyes to the plausibility of the charges he had made in "J'Accuse," and debate over the Dreyfus matter continued to rage unchecked. Zola himself was still free. He had appealed his conviction and, on the basis of a legal technicality, had won the right to a new trial. He and his friends had thereupon renewed their crusade to persuade public opinion; they had released a flood of revisionist pamphlets and dedicated Dreyfusards had traveled all over France to proclaim the urgent need for a new Dreyfus trial wherever they could find a platform. Their efforts had paid off. During the months following the Zola trial new recruits had flocked to join the Dreyfusard ranks. Hundreds upon hundreds of merchants, laborers, intellectuals, doctors, lawyers, rich men, poor men, Protestants, Jews and Catholics had come to see that justice was indivisible, that if one Frenchman were abandoned to the wolves of expediency, no Frenchman was safe.

Méline was no longer Premier. The national elections in May had returned a Parliament which, unable to agree among themselves on a score of other matters, had gotten together in June to turn Méline and his cabinet out. Henri Brisson, a Republican, became Premier and he, hoping to satisfy the still powerful Right, had named the nationalists' new favorite, General Godefroy Cavaignac, as his Minister of War. Pleased, the nationalists had sheathed their political daggers. They were confident that Cavaignac would do whatever was necessary to silence not only the annoying French revisionists, but the clamoring legions of foreign critics as well. Cavaignac had long railed against Billot's "vacillating" handling of the Dreyfus matter. If he were Minister of War,

he had said, he would finish off the Dreyfus Affair with a
"bludgeon stroke."

Soon after taking over the War Ministry, Cavaignac had
seen an opportunity to wield his bludgeon. The Deputy
Castelin announced his intention to question the government on why it allowed the distressing Dreyfusard agitation
to continue confusing the French people, and Cavaignac let
it be known that he would answer Castelin in the Chamber on
July 7.

Now, on the appointed day, the restless, perspiring
Deputies swatted at flies and consulted their watches as
they waited for Cavaignac to appear. Suddenly a door
opened and the War Minister strode to the speaker's stand.
It was obvious that Cavaignac considered himself a man
with a vital mission; his physique was slight but as he stood
waiting for Castelin's questions, he threw his chest out in an
attitude of supreme self-confidence. His long, lean face was
grave. His long, drooping mustache twitched portentously.
The Deputy Castelin got to his feet and put forth a formal
request to the government to inform the French people of the
truth concerning the Dreyfus matter and to, thereby, put an
end to the shameful commotion that was weakening the
country and making France ridiculous in the eyes of her
enemies. Castelin sat down and all eyes were glued on
Cavaignac as he started to speak.

France, Cavaignac said, was quite well able to take care
of her own affairs in her own way and he wished it understood that no part of what he was about to say was the
business of any foreigners. Applause. Good for Cavaignac!
Frenchmen were tired of outsiders telling them what to do
and how to do it. The general continued: It appeared that
there was reason to believe that Esterhazy was, after all,

implicated in the Dreyfus matter and he would be dealt with in good time. A startled murmur ran through the assemblage. But, Cavaignac hastened to add, Esterhazy's part in the affair in no way mitigated the absolute fact of Dreyfus's guilt. He, Cavaignac, was prepared to produce proof of that fact and he proposed to do so at once.

The general then read out loud to the attentive Deputies the entire texts of three documents from the heretofore supersecret Dreyfus file. The first was the famous "Scoundrel D." letter (no more relevant to Dreyfus now than it had ever been); the second was the note written by the Italian military attaché, Panizzardi, in which he asked his German counterpart, von Schwartzkoppen, to visit him "for D. has brought a number of interesting things" (this was the letter Henry had altered in 1896, erasing the original initial P. and writing a D. in its place); and the third document was the same one General Pellieux had spoken of during the Zola trial — the letter Henry had manufactured and then presented to General Gonse as a note from Panizzardi to von Schwartzkoppen saying in part, "I shall say I never had relations with this Jew . . . If you are asked, say the same thing, for no one must ever know what happened with him." Cavaignac sincerely believed in the authenticity of all three documents and his solemn assurances of their decisive nature so impressed the Deputies that they rose as one man to give the Minister a thunderous ovation. At last an end had been made to the Dreyfus Case! Now at last the insistent clamor for revision would be stilled. Now, finally, Parliament could turn its attention to the pressing matters that had been shoved aside in the continuing uproar over the Dreyfus Affair. Why had General Billot not had the courage to do what General Cavaignac had just done? Enthusiastically, the Deputies passed a unanimous vote to post Cavaignac's speech on the town hall of each of France's more than 35,000 communes.

The anti-Semitic and clerical newspapers crowed exultantly. Heaping lavish thanks on Cavaignac for his patriotic courage, they announced to the world that with a single stroke the general had given the lie to France's critics and restored shattered national confidence and unity.

But Georges Picquart had not been felled by Cavaignac's bludgeon. While in uniform, Picquart felt a duty to protect his superiors; now, however, disowned by the Army and wearing civilian clothes, he felt free to speak his mind. Two days after Cavaignac's speech, Picquart wrote a public letter to the Premier, Brisson, in which he branded Cavaignac's first two documents as "inapplicable to Dreyfus" and the third as a forgery. Furious, Cavaignac retaliated by arresting Picquart and imprisoning him in the military fortress of Mont-Valérien on the old charge of having communicated confidential military information to a civilian.

Now the voice of the revisionists could hardly be heard. In *L'Aurore* Clemenceau argued without letup for a new Dreyfus trial but *L'Aurore*'s circulation was pitifully small compared to that of the militantly anti-revisionist papers and Clemenceau's articles were read only by those he had already convinced. Picquart was in prison and Scheurer-Kestner lay seriously ill. And Zola? On the night of July 19 Zola fled France. At his second trial, held at Versailles the day before, he had received no fairer treatment than at his first and his attorneys had advised him to evade the prison sentence handed out by the second jury by going into exile. He could best serve the cause of revision, they said, by remaining at liberty and holding himself in readiness to return to France and take up the fight again when they notified him that the time was ripe. Zola hated the thought of running away but he allowed himself to be convinced and with a heavy heart he sailed for England. Once there he tried to forget the bitterness of his exile by plunging into preparations for a new novel but he found that literature had lost its allure for him; he could think of nothing but his country's plight and his days revolved around the arrival of the newspapers from France. Deeply depressed, he wrote to Labori:

> You would not believe the horror I feel at the echoes which reach me from France . . . We can no longer rely on justice . . . I have hope only in the unknown and the unexpected. What we need is a thunderbolt dropped from heaven, or else the slow workings of infinitely small events which will gradually gnaw through everything . . .

At the end of August Zola got his thunderbolt and, ironically, it was not a heavenly agent but General Cavaignac, himself, who hurled it. Cavaignac had not been able to rest easy; Picquart was in jail but the doubt he had cast on Cavaignac's "proofs" rankled. Eager to publicly refute Picquart's challenge, Cavaignac ordered one of his subordinates, a Captain Cuignet, to make a thorough examination of all the documents in the Dreyfus file with a view to establishing the absolute authenticity of each of them. The conscientious Captain Cuignet set to work and one evening in August, when he was examining the documents by lamplight, he happened to hold one of them up to the light and was startled to see that the paper on which it had been written bore one watermark at top and bottom and another in the middle. That the document was constructed of several pieces of paper pasted together was not at all remarkable — the bulk of Madame Bastian's wastepaper booty came to the Statistical Section in the form of torn-up scraps that had to be gummed together before the original message could be read — but a document made of fragments bearing different watermarks was obviously a dishonest reconstruction — in short, a forgery! When Cuignet hastened to show his discovery to Cavaignac, the general was horrified to see that the document was one of those he had spoken of in his July 7 speech and was the very one that Picquart had branded as a forgery. It was Colonel Henry who had "found" the letter in the War Office files and had brought it to General Gonse's attention and it was Henry, therefore, who must be called to account for it. Henry, however, was away on leave. Cavaignac, saying nothing of Cuignet's discovery to anyone else, swore the captain to secrecy and waited impatiently for Henry's return.

On August 30 Henry returned to Paris and answered a summons to appear at the War Minister's office. In General Boisdeffre's presence Cavaignac confronted him with the obviously forged document that he had given to General Gonse in 1896 as "overwhelming proof" of Dreyfus's guilt. At first Henry vehemently denied any tampering with the letter but finally, under Cavaignac's insistent questioning, he broke down and admitted that he had "doctored" it somewhat. Relentlessly, Cavaignac pressed him for details and at last they came out. The heading and the signature of the document were genuine pieces of Panizzardi's handwriting snipped from an unimportant note that the Italian attaché had written to von Schwartzkoppen and that, thanks to Madame Bastian, had subsequently fallen into the hands of the French Statistical Section. The body of the document, however, was false. The paper it was written on had originally been the blank end portion of another Panizzardi note. On this blank scrap a message, seemingly positively damning for Dreyfus but actually invented by Henry himself, had been forged in a skillful copy of Panizzardi's handwriting. Not noticing the difference in watermarks, Henry had then inserted and gummed the forged fragment between the genuine heading and signature. Pale and stammering, Henry assured Cavaignac that he had fabricated the document "for the good of the country."

A nightmare vision rose before General Cavaignac's eyes. He saw the bulletin boards of 35,000 French town halls, each bearing a copy of his speech in which he assured the country of the authenticity of the document Henry had just admitted having forged. Livid with rage, Cavaignac brushed aside Henry's attempts to explain further and ordered him to wait in an adjoining room. Turning to Boisdeffre, Cavaignac found the Chief of Staff seated at a desk, writing. After a moment, Boisdeffre put down his pen and wordlessly handed what he had written to Cavaignac:

> Sir: I have just received proof that my trust in Colonel Henry, head of the Intelligence Service, has not been justified. This trust, which was absolute, has led to my deception, and to my declaring to be genuine a piece which was not so, and to my handing it to you as such.
> In the circumstances, I have the honor to ask to be relieved of my duties.

Cavaignac did everything he could to dissuade Boisdeffre but Boisdeffre would not be moved. He was preoccupied with his own terrible mental image; in retrospect he saw himself standing before Zola's jury and giving them his word as

Chief of the General Staff that the document which Pellieux had said was proof of Dreyfus's guilt was unassailably authentic. No, he assured Cavaignac, he had no choice but to resign.

Henry was escorted to his home where he was permitted to pack some clothing and embrace his wife in farewell. He was then taken directly to the Mont-Valérien fortress.

The next day, August 31, dawned blazingly hot. The new prisoner asked his guards for copies of the day's newspapers and when they were given to him he searched their columns for reason to hope that all was not lost for him. Were there any statements of support from the generals whose interests his forgery had served so well? There were none. He had been abandoned. In the middle of the afternoon Henry started a note to his wife by saying, "I see that, except for you, everyone is going to desert me . . ." He assured her that he had been misjudged, that he was actually innocent of all wrongdoing. Later in the afternoon he wrote to his wife again, "My beloved Berthe, I feel quite mad, a terrible pain is pressing my skull, I am going to take a bathe in the Seine . . ." Sometime after that, and before six o'clock in the evening, Henry lay down on his cot and cut his throat with his razor. A prison attendant, bringing his supper to his cell, found his dead body.

That evening Esterhazy received word of Henry's suicide and promptly started to pack. Early the next morning he boarded a train for Mauberge on the Belgian border. At Mauberge he shaved off his mustache, slipped across the border on foot and proceeded from Belgium to London where he went into hiding under the name of Monsieur de Bécourt.

COLONEL HENRY ARRESTED ON CHARGES OF FORGERY! CHIEF OF GENERAL STAFF RESIGNS! HENRY A SUICIDE IN PRISON!

ESTERHAZY FLEES FRANCE! Following one after the other in rapid succession, big black headlines blared out the news that the Dreyfus Case, declared by the highest government and Army officials to be firmly closed, had blown wide open again. Incredulous Frenchmen snatched newspapers from newsboys' hands, pored over press accounts of the stupefying new developments and tried to analyze their implications. Henry's confession that he had forged one document pointed inexorably to the strong possibility that he had forged others. Was not Esterhazy's flight tantamount to an admission of guilt? Surely, honest men must now look at Zola's "J'Accuse" in a new light. Was the man who had already walked the hot sands of Devil's Island for more than three long years an innocent after all? All over France men who had placed implicit trust in the word of the generals now shook their heads in shock and dismay. Reluctantly, many of them came to the conclusion that only a thorough review of the whole muddy Dreyfus Case could pull France from the quicksands of intrigue and deception in which she foundered. Revision! Revision! In the days that followed Henry's suicide thousands upon thousands of new voices called out for a new trial for Alfred Dreyfus.

Rejoicing over the new turn of events in France, and confident that Henry's confession had cleared the path to revision, Zola prepared to return to France. A letter from Labori, however, stopped him. Labori was not so optimistic; he was afraid that there were still hard times ahead and he advised Zola to remain in England.

Labori was right. Premier Brisson was among those convinced by the exposure of the Henry forgery that revision was inevitable, but when he suggested to General Cavaignac that the War Ministry should set the revision process in motion the general balked. Stubbornly refusing to admit that he had been completely hoodwinked, Cavaignac reasoned around the awkward facts of Henry's crime. He told Brisson that the exposure of one of the documents in the Dreyfus file as a fraud did not detract from the validity of the others. He insisted that since Henry's forgery had been perpetrated two years after Dreyfus had been convicted, it did not in any way alter the fact of Dreyfus's guilt and he declared himself as firmly opposed to revision as ever. When Brisson pressed him he resigned and announced that he would assume the leadership of the fight to prevent a new trial.

Laid low by the shattering effects of Henry's confession and suicide, the nationalists took heart on hearing of Cavaignac's obstinate espousal of their cause and they hastened to line up behind him. Nothing has changed, they shouted. Dreyfus is still guilty. The Army's honor must still be defended at all costs. A grossly retouched picture of the dead Henry began to emerge from the pages of the Catholic and anti-Semitic press: Henry was not the dastardly scoundrel his forgery had at first made him seem; on the contary, he had acted as a great patriot and had died as a martyr! According to the yellow press, Henry had fabricated his "proof" of Dreyfus's guilt for the express purpose of relieving his superiors of the necessity of producing their genuine proofs — documents which, if publicly exposed, would have led to immediate and disastrous war with Germany. Charles Maurras, a leading spokesman for the nationalists, piously claimed that Henry had forged "for the public welfare" and added, "our defective education, half Protestant, is incapable of appreciating such intellectual and moral nobility."

Beguiled by rationalizations they wanted to believe, many

Frenchmen were persuaded to see a through-the-looking-glass image of reality; the confessed forger was not a criminal but a hero; the Dreyfusards' talk of liberty and justice was no more than a smokescreen put up to confuse and mislead the unwary; the military leaders who continued to insist on Dreyfus's guilt were neither stubborn nor stupid, they were astute. Assured by their newspapers that only continuing hatred for the Jews, suspicion of "misguided intellectuals" and blind trust in the Army could cure France's ills, the public docilely took the medicine the nationalists prescribed. As national tension mounted, long-quiescent Royalist and Bonapartist factions stirred and rallied their supporters. Rumors of impending uprisings and coups d'état swept through Paris.

Brisson was in a very tight spot. With Cavaignac in his cabinet he had been able to appease the Right; without Cavaignac, his hold on Parliament's confidence was shaky at best. Afraid to move for revision lest he be censured for "meddling in military affairs," Brisson tried to find a new Minister of War who would so move. His first choice, General Zurlinden, preferred to busy himself with seeking reprisals against Picquart for his "disloyalty to the Army." Zurlinden had shuffled Picquart, the petit bleu and the Henry forgery and had come up with a new combination. Picquart, said Zurlinden, had forged the famous petit bleu for the purpose of pinning Dreyfus's crime on Esterhazy and Henry had thereupon fabricated his "patriotic forgery" in order to offset Picquart's deception. The general was, however, willing to throw one lamb to the Dreyfusard wolves. When Du Paty admitted to a commission of inquiry that he had made contact with Esterhazy without the knowledge of his superior officers, Zurlinden ordered the major retired on half-pay. But he would go no further. When Brisson urged him to turn his attention to revision, he resigned. Brisson, still not daring to take it upon himself to start the revision process, advised Lucie Dreyfus to make an independent application for a review of her husband's case and then he turned back to his search for a more amenable War Minister.

In General Chanoine, Brisson thought he had found his man. But, shortly after his arrival at the War Ministry, Chanoine double-crossed his Premier. First he took up Zurlinden's vendetta against Picquart and then, soon after Lucie Dreyfus had filed an application for revision through the Ministry of Justice, he precipitated a cabinet crisis which forced Brisson and his cabinet to resign.

Paris seethed with unrest. Subway construction workers who had gone out on strike for reasons of their own were infiltrated by nationalist agitators. Royalist and Bonapartist hoodlums joined anti-Semitic gangs and roamed the streets provoking brawls wherever they could. The government, fearing a popular uprising at any moment, sent troops to occupy the city's railroad stations. Rumors snowballed. One day Parisians heard that Dreyfus was dead and the next day they heard that not only was he very much alive but that he had escaped from Devil's Island. By the time that rumor was officially squelched, the city had heard another — Zola, it was said, was living a life of luxurious ease in England financed by international Jewry. Suspicion and doubt ruled over France with an iron hand and revision, so excitingly imminent at the beginning of September, seemed, by the end of the month, as far away as ever.

14

The Courts Speak

AT THE END of October Dreyfusard hopes soared again. Lucie Dreyfus's application for a review of her husband's case had come before the Criminal Court of Appeals, the criminal chamber of the nation's highest appellate court, and on October 29 the sixteen-judge bench ruled that the application had enough merit to warrant further investigation. Tentative as this legal pronouncement was, it raised a storm of excitement. Hailed with jubilant delight on one side it was denounced angrily on the other. Now a new trial is certain, Dreyfusards assured each other; now, said the nationalists, this insidious campaign for revision must be choked off once and for all.

The anti-Semitic and anti-Republic press peppered the judges of the Criminal Court with threats and accusations. A succession of glaring headlines announced that the judges had shown a scandalous lack of respect for the 1894 military verdict and shocking partiality to Dreyfusard witnesses. In *L'Intransigeant* Rochefort solemnly recommended excruciating physical torture as the only fit punishment for men who, claiming to be jurists, were actually "stooges of the Jewish Syndicate." When, shortly after handing down its ruling, the court added insult to the nationalists' injury by insisting that Dreyfus be informed that his case was again before the courts, the howls from the anti-revisionist camp grew louder and more anguished. Drumont assured the readers of *La Libre Parole* that there could be only one explanation for the court's solicitous concern for a traitor's peace of mind — "Jewish money."

Resolutely refusing to be intimidated, the sixteen judges began the investigation they had ruled advisable. As insults and threats continued to fly about their heads they called a parade of witnesses and subpoenaed the War Office's top-secret file on Dreyfus. When they listened sympathetically to Picquart's story optimism flooded through the revisionist camp. When they expressed surprise at the hollowness of the Army's secret dossier it seemed certain to Dreyfusard and anti-Dreyfusard alike that the sixteen jurists would conclude their investigation by ruling for a new trial. Desperate now, the nationalists launched an all-out attack on the Criminal Court. Their hope was to so discredit the court that the Dreyfus matter would be removed from its jurisdiction and placed before a "United Court" made up of the three high appeals chambers which, the nationalists thought, would be more susceptible to pressure from the Right.

CRIMINAL JUDGES SOLD TO SYNDICATE! FATE OF FRANCE IN HANDS OF 16 CORRUPT JUDGES! TRAITOR JUDGES BOW TO JEWS! Each day the nationalist papers overflowed with sensational stories of judicial corruption and sinister behind-the-scenes intrigues that threatened the peace and well-being of every Frenchman. Before long the nationalist editors achieved their first objective. The public, persuaded to believe that where there was so much smoke there must be at least a little fire, gave strong support to a "people's movement" that called for the transfer of the Dreyfus appeal from the Criminal Court where it properly belonged to an unprecedented three-chamber United Court of Appeals.

The new Premier, Charles Dupuy, was not a fool and he must have known that if the government bowed to irresponsible press attacks on one court, no court would be safe. But Dupuy was afraid; he feared that if he defended the maligned judges he would be tarred with the same anti-Semitic brush that was blackening them. Seeking to avoid the responsibility for making a decision, Dupuy set up a committee of eminent jurists to examine the charges made against the Criminal Court. He hoped that the committee would clear the judges of all suspicion of malpractice and so still the clamor for a United Court. He was disappointed. The committee did refute the nationalists' charges of bribery but it also recommended that the Criminal Court be relieved of the responsibility for deciding on such an "extraordinary" matter, a matter which the committee said, could best be handled by an "extraordinary" United Court. Dupuy made no further effort to uphold the competence of the beleaguered Criminal Court. On January 30 a government bill proposing that the three Appeals Courts sit together to consider the Dreyfus appeal was placed before the Chamber of Deputies.

A few Deputies recognized the ominous threat to democratic government contained in the proposed bill and fought to prevent its becoming law. The Socialist Deputy Millerand warned the Chamber that clerical and anti-Semitic editors were already "drawing up denunciations of other courts, to have judges outlawed because this one is a Jew, the other a Protestant, the next one the brother of a revisionist." But the Deputies turned deaf ears to Millerand and listened instead to Lebret, the Minister of Justice, who reminded them that if they wished to be re-elected to their seats in the Chamber they would do well to reflect the wishes of an aroused electorate. "Look to your constituencies," Lebret warned, and the

Chamber, bowing to the pressure of inflamed public opinion, passed the bill and sent it to the Senate for final action.

Observers all over the world were shocked. Ever since Zola's trial it had seemed to them that Frenchmen were literally throwing away their proud and dearly bought democratic heritage. Now it appeared that the French Republic might receive a mortal blow in the very legislative assemblies designed to preserve it. The French people, however, beguiled by myths and persuaded to fear enemies that did not exist, were unaware of the real danger that threatened them. Surrounded on all sides by the Dreyfus Affair, they were at a loss to understand it.

In Paris, society wrangled interminably about the Affair. Finding themselves unable to agree on the question of Dreyfus's guilt, once-loving sisters and brothers, parents and children stopped speaking to one another; betrothals were abruptly broken off by parents who could not see eye to eye on the Affair with their prospective in-laws; bitter arguments dissolved long-standing business associations; fashionable hostesses invited their friends to dinner with the assurance that "the Dreyfus Case will positively not be discussed." Ironically, a few educated, wealthy Jews were now welcomed in exclusive circles from which their Jewishness had previously barred them. Why? The Affair. The Affair had endowed all Jews with an aura of sinister intrigue that had a strong attraction for many of the bored and sensation-hungry rich. Some of the newly favored Jews were fooled. Others, more realistic, were not; they recognized the source of their sudden acceptability for what it was — highly sophisticated anti-Semitism.

Preoccupation with the Affair was not confined to society.

Housewives got the fishmonger's opinion of Zola and Picquart with their fish; workingmen skipped their suppers to
discuss the latest batch of rumors in neighborhood bistros;
teen-age boys broke out in a rash of black eyes and bloodied
noses acquired in street-corner "Dreyfus brawls"; in the sidewalk cafés university students argued over their pernods
while pretty young women paraded past unnoticed. And
every day *La Libre Parole* replenished the city's stock of exciting rumors and speculations about the menacing power of
the "international Jewish Syndicate."

FOR THE WIDOW AND ORPHAN OF COLONEL HENRY AGAINST
THE JEW REINACH! In December *La Libre Parole*'s Drumont
seized on what he saw as a golden opportunity to not only
inflate the image of the dead Colonel Henry as a "selfless
martyr" but also to provoke new outbursts of hostility against
the Jews. Henry's widow had come to him requesting financial assistance. She wished to sue Joseph Reinach for writing
an article which she thought defamed the memory of her
husband but she lacked the funds to do so. Drumont was
happy to help her. Through his paper he launched a vast
fund-raising campaign and money began to pour in at once.
Each day Drumont printed the names of the latest contributors together with the hate-crazed messages that accompanied their donations. Within a month's time 130,000 francs
($26,000) was received from fifteen thousand French citizens
who expressed wishes to see all French Jews barred from
public office or deprived of their citizenship rights, or de-
ported, or stripped of all their possessions, or tossed in the
Seine or a combination of several of these. A considerable
number of the messages were unprintable but Drumont
printed them with the rest. The bulk of the money raised
came from uneducated Frenchmen who, if they could read

at all, read only *La Libre Parole* and believed every word
Drumont printed, but also included among the contributors
were hundreds of aristocrats, more than a thousand active
and retired Army officers, four Senators, and fifty-three
Deputies. General Mercier sent 100 francs.

Shocked by the worsening turn of events in France, Albert,
the ruling Prince of the tiny principality of Monaco, decided
that he must do something to help his French neighbors re-
gain their senses. He had already gone to the assistance of
two Frenchmen who had dared to speak out against injustice
and had been ruined for their trouble. When Forzinetti had
repeated his belief in Dreyfus's innocence once too often
and had been discharged from his post as Commandant of
the Cherche-Midi prison, Albert had given him a job as a
civil servant in Monaco; when a French abbé had been disowned by his parishioners for counseling brotherly love for
non-Catholics, he too had found asylum in Monaco. Now,
however, Albert hoped to help France herself. It occurred to
him that since Monaco was, because of its size, definitely outside the arena of European power politics, he might act as a
neutral intermediary between France and Germany and in
that way help France to get at the truth underlying her
multiplying difficulties. Accordingly, he requested an interview with Félix Faure, the President of France, and on the
afternoon of February 16, 1899, Faure received him at the
Elysée, the presidential palace.

Faure was polite but noncommittal. He must have recognized that Albert's intentions were friendly but if he thought
that the Prince could be of any real assistance to France he
gave no indication of it. The interview came to an inconclusive end and Albert was ushered out. Somewhat later in

the afternoon Faure received another visitor, a Madame Steinheil, who was shown into the private presidential suite of offices. At 6:45 strangled cries were heard from Faure. An aide, rushing to his side, found him in the throes of a cerebral seizure. Doctors were called but Faure was beyond help. By ten o'clock that evening he was dead. Because Madame Steinheil was still with the President at the time of his seizure, the circumstances surrounding his death were hushed up and the public was free to speculate as to what had caused it. The nationalist press lost no time. MURDER! JEWISH-HIRED ASSASSINS! THE SYNDICATE AT WORK! One newspaper editor, claiming inside information, laid Faure's death at the door of Albert of Monaco; Albert, he said, had given Faure a poisoned cigarette.

The news of Faure's sudden, mysterious death honed public tension to a sharp edge. Already upset and confused by the continuing turmoil surrounding the Dreyfus Affair, Parisians now found that everywhere they turned they heard rumors of conspiracies to kill other French leaders and plots to overthrow the government. As a pall of fear and uncertainty descended over the city, long quiescent advocates of totalitarian rule decided that now if ever the time was ripe for upheaval. While Parliament met hurriedly at Versailles to elect Faure's successor, militarist conspirators plotted to make a grab for power on the occasion of Faure's funeral. Their candidate for military dictator was General Pellieux.

The President of the Senate, Emile Loubet, a Republican and a staunch pro-revisionist, was elected President of France over vehement protests from the Right. On his way from Versailles to the Elysée he was hooted at by anti-Semitic ruffians posted along his route but he remained unruffled. "The Republic will not founder in my hands," he said, "they know it and it maddens them."

On February 23, Paris turned out en masse to watch the pomp and ceremony of a presidential funeral. Loubet and high-ranking members of the government led the procession. They were followed by General Pellieux astride a prancing horse riding at the head of a parade of troops. The scene was impressive. The soldiers stepped out smartly, flags flew, bands played funeral dirges and patriotic anthems. Emotional spectators, their nerves rubbed raw by snowballing rumors about the circumstances of Faure's death, alternately wept in grief for their dead President and cheered in pride of their glorious Army. The atmosphere was tight with tension and the situation was made to order for a coup d'état.

But conspiratorial ineptness, a reluctant general and a skittish horse came between the insurrectionists and their goal. General Pellieux, informed only that morning that he was to be swept to supreme power by nightfall, decided on the way to the cemetery that the risks involved were greater than he cared to take. On the way back he led his own battalion away from the appointed rendezvous with the conspirators at the Place de la Nation and left the main body of troops to proceed along the announced parade route under the command of his subordinate, General Roget, who knew nothing of the plot. When the troops hove into view at the Place de la Nation, the band of two hundred waiting conspirators were taken aback to see that the general in command was not Pellieux but Roget. A hurried decision was taken: Roget would have to do. A group of men broke through the crowd of spectators, rushed up to Roget and called on him to save France and to follow them in a march on the presidential palace. The general's horse, frightened by the sudden foray, reared and bucked. A military band marching behind Roget struck up the "Marseillaise." The blaring music all but drowned out the shouts of the men running alongside Roget's horse and the general, unable to catch the gist of what they were saying, ignored them and concentrated all his energies on staying in the saddle. The insurrectionist leaders persisted. They ran after Roget, pleading with him to help them overthrow the Republic. The general, still uncomprehending, and by this time thoroughly annoyed, tried to lead his troops past them. Arriving at the military barracks with the militarists still in pursuit, Roget had their leaders arrested. Outside the barracks, the crowds whom the insurrectionists had hoped to stampede into shouting "Down with the Republic!" lustily shouted "Long Live the Republic!" instead and went home.

Four days later the Senate met to vote on the government bill proposing that the Dreyfus appeal be referred to a United Court of Appeals. A small group of Republican Senators struggled to defeat the bill. Addressing the Senators on the Right, Pierre Waldeck-Rousseau said:

> We Frenchmen were once hungry for justice. Now it has been possible to declare, and without a shudder running through the whole country, that a reason of state can outweigh justice to the individual. You talk of [public] opinion. I answer; let us talk of justice.

The Senators, however, hungered more for votes than for justice. Passing the bill by a majority of twenty, they completed Parliament's surrender to the demands of a nationalist-inflamed society. The question of revision was now formally placed before the forty-six justices of a United Court of Appeals.

Rejoicing at their victory over the "partial" Criminal Court, the nationalists settled back to await the verdict of the United Court, a verdict which they felt sure would put a final end to the campaign for revision. It seemed that they had every reason for confidence. During the four years just past they had made ever deeper penetrations of the Republic's defenses. Holding the threat of parliamentary censure over the heads of each successive ministry, the military–clerical–anti-Semitic alliance had bent each government to its will; Parliament itself had just capitulated to nationalist pressure. The Criminal Court had tried to buck the tide of public opinion and had failed; surely the United Court would avoid the Criminal Court's error.

But, lusting for final victory, the nationalists failed to see that the sixteen judges of the Criminal Court had triumphed even as they had gone down in defeat. Their courageous stand for justice had infused their fellow jurists with courage. As the forty-six judges of the United Court of Appeals began their investigation of the Dreyfus Case they gave no indication of being any more amenable than the smaller court had been. They, too, called a host of witnesses and gave them fair hearings; they, too, commandeered the secret Dreyfus file and, on examining it, expressed shock at its lack of substance. Under their direction France was scoured for new evidence and under their orders appeals went out for all who had knowledge of the Dreyfus Case to come forward and be heard.

Two men of troubled conscience heeded the court's appeal. The first was one of the handwriting experts who had branded Dreyfus as the author of the bordereau in 1894; he told the United Court that if he had seen samples of Esterhazy's writing then he would have testified that Esterhazy, not Dreyfus, had written the document. The second was a Captain Freystatter, one of the court-martial judges who had convicted Dreyfus in 1894; Freystatter told the judges that Colonel Henry's confession of forgery and subsequent suicide had led him to seriously doubt the justice of the verdict he had helped to bring about. Upon being questioned Freystatter revealed that it had been Colonel Henry's sworn statement that Dreyfus was the traitor the War Office was seeking that had convinced him he should vote for a verdict of guilty; that after the exposure of Henry's duplicity he had been haunted night and day by the thought of a possibly innocent man suffering the torment of exile on Devil's Island; that he had delayed reentering the case for fear of displeasing his superiors and that he had finally done so because his conscience would allow him no rest. Freystatter wound up his testimony by admitting that in 1894 he and his fellow court-martial judges had examined secret evidence that had not been shown to the defense.

At about the same time a discrepancy between the files of the War Office and those of the Foreign Office came to light. The contradiction concerned the text of the telegram sent in 1894 by Panizzardi, the Italian military attaché in Paris, to his home office in Rome and intercepted and decoded by the French Foreign Office. A representative of the Foreign Office, Maurice Paléologue, told the court that the message had been a simple request by Panizzardi to his superiors for an official denial of press reports concerning their contacts with Dreyfus if they had had no dealings with him. According to a spokesman for the War Office, however,

the text of the telegram implied Dreyfus's guilt; he said
that it read: "Dreyfus arrested. Precautions taken. Emissary
warned." To settle the dispute the court ordered the Foreign
Office to produce the original tracing of the intercepted code
message and to re-decode it in court. When this was done
and the resulting message was read out loud in court it was
painfully clear that Paléologue had been quite right when
he had said: "The version in the War Office file is not only
erroneous, it is false."

Finally, after eighty witnesses had been heard and 1168
pages in the court record had been filled with notations, the
United Court prepared to hear the three crucial presenta-
tions on which it would base its final verdict — a summary
of both sides of the case to be presented by one of the
justices of the Court, Judge Ballot-Beaupré, a statement by
the prosecution and another by the defense. After hearing
these the Court would have to decide either to uphold the
1894 verdict, or to annul it and free Dreyfus without further
legal proceedings, or to annul the original verdict and
order Dreyfus to stand a retrial before a court-martial jury.

On May 29 both Ballot-Beaupré and the prosecuting attorney told the Court that they believed enough evidence
pointing to Dreyfus's innocence had been uncovered to
warrant an annulment of the 1894 verdict. The packed
courtroom rang with Dreyfusard applause and then quieted
suddenly as Lucie Dreyfus's attorney, Henry Mornard, rose
to speak. He, too, he said, fervently desired an annulment
of the old verdict but he was compelled to request something
more:

> . . . In accordance with the orders of my client, gentle-
> men, I have been obliged to recommend that the case
> be remanded to a court-martial . . . I query whether it

would not, in truth, have been more humane to move
that the judgement be set aside without remand, as it
was my right to do. But, in any event, I want to have it
clearly understood that, if I have urged remanding the
case to a court-martial, that was because I was obliged
to yield to the very honorable sentiments expressed in
Captain Dreyfus's letters. Dreyfus was dispossessed of
his honor through the error of his brothers in arms. It
is for those brothers in arms to return that honor to
him. It is before them that he wishes to appear.

At the conclusion of Mornard's remarks the court adjourned
and the judges retired to deliberate on what they had heard.

Five days later the court delivered its ruling: on the basis
of several "new facts," one of the most important of which
was proof of an illegal communication of secret evidence to
the 1894 court-martial, the 1894 verdict was annulled and
the Dreyfus Case was referred to a military court-martial in
the city of Rennes for retrial in August. The forty-six judges
made it plain that they all believed in Dreyfus's innocence
and that it was only in order to accede to the defense's
request for a new trial that they had left one question open:
did Dreyfus write the bordereau and give the items of information listed in it to enemy agents?

Revision at last! Mathieu and Lucie Dreyfus wept for
joy and Dreyfusards all over the world rejoiced. In London,
Emile Zola trembled with excitement as he prepared to take
the next boat for France; Georges Picquart, still in prison,
looked forward to an early release; and in Biarritz, a
dying man, Senator Scheurer-Kestner, wrote to his daughter,
Jeanne:

You ask me if I am happy? How many men are

there who, after they have sacrificed themselves to a just cause, witness the triumph of that cause?

I am blessed beyond the ordinary, and I am keenly aware of it. True, I have said to myself on occasion that I have paid dearly, at the price of my health. But I say this without regret. If I should be offered the good health I enjoyed before the Affair, in return for defeat, leaving poor Dreyfus on Devil's Island, I should refuse that offer . . . It is . . . pleasant to think that I shall leave to my grandchildren an honorable name. That will prolong my life a generation and, since I am very fond of life, I am content . . .

Far across the vast stretches of the Atlantic Ocean another Frenchman first heard of the United Court's decision on June 5. At a little after noon on that day the chief guard on Devil's Island walked into Alfred Dreyfus's hut and handed him a dispatch which began:

> Please let Captain Dreyfus know immediately of this order of the Supreme Court. The Court quashes and annuls the sentence pronounced on the 22nd of December, 1894 . . .

Eagerly, Dreyfus scanned the remainder of the message:

> . . . the Court . . . remands the accused party to a court-martial at Rennes . . . Captain Dreyfus becomes a simple prisoner under arrest and is restored to his rank and allowed to resume his uniform . . . the cruiser SFAX leaves Fort-de-France today with orders to take the prisoner from the island and bring him back to France . . .

Dreyfus had waited for this ever since the middle of November when he had first heard that his case was before the courts. His body wasted by fever and his nerves crushed under the weight of inhuman treatment and never-ending loneliness, he had for seven long months fed his will to survive on visions and dreams. As the days and weeks dragged past with no further official word, only his body remained in contact with the harsh realities of life on Devil's Island; his mind escaped into an imaginary world where truth was in the process of triumphantly breaking through the dark clouds of injustice that had enveloped him for so long. It seemed to him that his former military superiors must be behind the effort to save his honor and in his mind's eye he pictured General Boisdeffre working night and day to push forward the fight to rescue him. He dreamed of a telegraphed summons and a triumphant return to his homeland; he saw his wife and children waiting with open arms on the pier; he envisioned scenes in which his comrades-in-arms, weeping, begged his forgiveness for the terrible error that had been committed.

Now the telegram he held in his hand seemed proof that all his dreams were about to come true. He had no doubt but that the United Court had firmly established his innocence and that the court-martial at Rennes was to be held solely for the purpose of making official reparation for the previous court-martial's judicial error. Happiness flooding over him, Dreyfus took up his pen and, with tears of joy streaming from his eyes, he wrote out a telegram to be sent to his wife: "My heart and soul are with you, with my children, with my friends . . . I leave Friday. I wait with uncontrollable joy for the moment of supreme happiness when I shall hold you in my arms."

Section

IV

A KIND OF JUSTICE

Clouded Prospects

No SOONER had Dreyfus's friends recovered from their first excitement over the ruling for revision than they had started to discuss his chances for justice at Rennes. Now, three weeks after the United Court had handed down its decision, the debate still raged. Some Dreyfusards, encouraged by recent developments, were ready to bet their last francs on a speedy acquittal. As many others, however, were sadly convinced that the court-martial would recondemn.

An incident at the Auteuil racetrack on June 4 had led to the downfall of Charles Dupuy's government. Upon his arrival at Auteuil for an afternoon of relaxation and pleasure, Emile Loubet, the President of France, found himself the target of a demonstration staged by a band of hotheaded young Royalists protesting the revision ruling of the day before. Because most Frenchmen, whatever their political beliefs, admired Loubet for his rise from humble origins and his reputation for personal integrity, the crowd of fashionably dressed racing fans resented the aristocratic hoodlums' jeers and loud demands that Loubet resign. A scuffle broke out and in the midst of the ensuing confusion one brash young Royalist had the effrontery to force his way into the presidential box and strike at Loubet with his cane. Loubet suffered no greater injury than having his top hat knocked over his eyes and his assailant was promptly overpowered by indignant onlookers, but newspaper accounts of the incident enraged the general public. Why had the police not prevented the attack? What a disgrace it was that the President of France should lack proper protection! Overnight Loubet's popularity soared and, clasping their President to their hearts, thousands of French citizens previously opposed to the government now embraced the Republic he symbolized as well. Blame for Loubet's exposure to insult and attack was placed squarely on Dupuy's shoulders. Dupuy, it was said, did not care enough for the Republic to protect its President.

Dupuy was already in trouble with Parliament on several other counts but the Auteuil incident was the straw that broke his political back. On June 12 he resigned. How fickle the French people were! Only seven months earlier Dupuy's predecessor, Brisson, had fallen because Parliament thought him too zealous in his defense of Republican principles; now Dupuy had been forced to resign because he was considered to be not sufficiently pro-Republic.

The Chamber of Deputies gave the new Premier, René Waldeck-Rousseau, a hard time when he presented his cabinet for their approval. The Deputies on the Left approved of the staunchly Republican character of most of the ministers he had chosen and they applauded his promise to allow no government interference in the conduct of the trial at Rennes, but they took vociferous exception to his choice of War Minister, General Galliffet. The Deputies on the Right were much more critical; they angrily insisted that Waldeck-Rousseau had chosen "a Dreyfus Cabinet." After hours of heated argument in the Chamber a compromise measure was proposed and passed. The Deputies voted to adjourn for three months; the effect was to give Waldeck-

Rousseau and his cabinet a three-month period of grace. It was assumed that by the end of that time the Dreyfus Affair would be settled once and for all and that then, the political atmosphere unclouded by bias for or against Dreyfus, the Chamber would be able to consider the merits of the new government with judicious detachment.

In the meantime, the French public had become irritated by the nationalist newspapers' incessant attacks on the nation's courts. Six months earlier, a great many Frenchmen had found it possible to believe that the sixteen judges of the Criminal Court had sold their votes but when Drumont claimed in *La Libre Parole* that all forty-six judges of the United Court had also been bribed, his readers scoffed derisively. And when, on June 9, a lower court freed Picquart after he had served 325 days in prison, the nationalist press was unable to whip up even a small public protest.

All this certainly augured well for Alfred Dreyfus. Why then did many Dreyfusards see the future in a gloomy light? One thing that worried them was a newly intensified campaign of calumny against the Jews in the yellow press.

Nationalist editors, finding the public unreceptive to direct attacks on the government and the courts, had set out to convince their readers that at Rennes a final choice would have to be made between the Jews and France herself. If the court-martial found Dreyfus innocent, they said, then all those who had accused him, high-ranking Army officers and Cabinet Ministers, would have to be declared guilty; if this awful possibility became a reality, they added, the proud French nation would be forced to bow down to Jews all over the world and beg their pardon. Similar false simplifications of the issues to be faced at Rennes were dressed up in patriotic garb and sprinkled liberally in the clerical, anti-

General Jean-Baptiste Billot, General Mercier's successor as Minister of War

Georges Clemenceau, speaking on the Dreyfus Affair at a public meeting

(*Culver Pictures, Inc.*)

Emile Zola

Lieutenant Colonel Georges Picquart testifying at Zola's trial

Fernand Labori

Edouard Drumont, editor of the newspaper, *La Libre Parole*

Dreyfus shortly after his return from Devil's Island, at his trial at
Rennes

Courtroom scene during Dreyfus's trial at Rennes

Dreyfus and his children, Jeanne and Pierre, about 1901

Semitic and Army-inspired newspapers. There was no mention of the principles of justice for the individual and equality for all citizens. Instead there was this from *La Croix:*

> The question is not whether this wretch is guilty or innocent, but whether or not the Jews and the Protestants — this vanguard of Germany, England and their allies — are to rule our country . . .

and this from *La Libre Parole:*

> The court-martial will send Dreyfus back to Devil's Island and his arrival there will be the signal for the exodus of all Jews — voluntary or forced.

It was General Mercier, however, who worried pessimistic Dreyfusards the most. They knew that the United Court had backed Mercier into an extremely tight corner by citing the illegal communication of secret evidence to the 1894 court-martial as one of its reasons for ruling for revision; since it was common knowledge that Mercier was responsible for that communication, the court had, in effect, accused Mercier of a heinous crime. Could he avoid having to answer for that crime? Yes, if, and only if, the Rennes court-martial ruled that Dreyfus had, in fact, been guilty of treason. Then, and only then, Mercier's illegal act of 1894 could be seen, not as a crime, but as the courageous action of a dedicated Minister of War who had not hesitated to use "unconventional means" to save France from the evil machinations of her enemies. So, argued gloomy Dreyfusards, it was only realistic to assume that Mercier would lash out at Dreyfus at Rennes with all the ferocity of a wounded animal at bay, that he would stop at nothing to ensure Dreyfus's second conviction. Zola feared that they were right. The specter of a desperate Mercier, aided by subordinates whose fates were tied up with his, had been haunting him for a long time. Six months earlier, while he was still in exile in England, Zola had written to Labori:

> We have often said, in speaking of the bandits who are our adversaries, "they would not dare!" And they have always dared. So why should they not dare the worst crime of all, the stifling of truth, the condemnation of an innocent man for the second time? ... You will see, they will put out the sun. They would prefer eternal night to descend on the universe if it would cover up their crime.

Even the least hopeful Dreyfusards admitted that Mercier would not find it so easy to convince the court-martial of Dreyfus's guilt this time; he would not have the assistance of a compliant government as he had had in 1894. Nevertheless, as the time for the Rennes court-martial neared, there was no indication that Mercier was worried. On the contrary, he appeared supremely self-confident. He publicly announced his firm conviction that Dreyfus would be recondemned. The Army's proofs of Dreyfus's guilt, he said, were now more overwhelming than ever. Reporters calling at the War Ministry received dark hints concerning a hitherto undisclosed document proving Dreyfus's treason beyond all doubt. This document, the newsmen heard, was so explosive that General Mercier carried it around in his breast pocket lest it fall into the hands of those unfriendly to France. Soon it was rumored that the document in question was the original bordereau from which the bordereau produced in court in 1894 had been traced; this original, according to widely circulated reports, bore in its margins notations referring to Dreyfus written in the hand of none other than the German Kaiser! General Mercier would not confirm the reports. Neither would he deny them.

At about the same time Alfred Dreyfus, knowing nothing of the turmoil his case had aroused in France, was being assailed by a sudden gnawing anxiety about his future. On first hearing of the United Court's ruling for revision, he had joyfully jumped to the conclusion that the court had proven his innocence and that his second trial was to be held for the sole purpose of officially declaring it to the world. But on boarding the cruiser *Sfax*, he had been stricken with doubts. The ship's officers had treated him with chilly reserve and he had found that with the exception of an hour's deck privileges each morning and evening, he was to sit out the long voyage to France locked in his cabin. And yet, desperately clinging to his cherished belief that his torment was all but at an end, he had managed to rationalize away his misgivings. He was, after all, he reminded himself, still a prisoner and, therefore, the officers of the *Sfax* were entirely correct in treating him as such; the moment of his actual return to French soil would mark the beginning of a new and wonderful life for him and his family; his wife and children would be waiting at the pier; his brother officers, perhaps even General Boisdeffre himself would also be there to welcome him and to beg his forgiveness for the terrible error that had cost him so much suffering. Yes, that was how it would be. Unable to face the possibility that all might not turn out as he had pictured it, Dreyfus had built an impregnable barricade around his high hopes and had patiently waited out the long days at sea.

But cruel disillusionment lay in wait for Dreyfus. On

June 30, a day of heavy rain and high seas, the *Sfax* sighted the coast of France. Her engines stopped and after a long unexplained wait the prisoner was fetched and put into a small boat for transfer to a steam launch lying at anchor nearby. During his four and a half years on Devil's Island Dreyfus had become accustomed to the torrid heat of the tropics and as he sat in the open boat, exposed to the cold wind and icy rain, he was seized with a violent chill. As the boat alternately rose to dizzy heights and plunged precipitously into the deep valleys between the waves, he writhed in an agony of seasickness. On reaching the launch, Dreyfus, shivering and ill, asked her captain to which point on the French coast she would head and when he was sternly told that he could not be given that information his heart sank. The launch's engines started up and she steamed ahead for a short time and then stopped. No explanation was given to Dreyfus but, after an hour had passed and the launch continued to lie at anchor, he realized that the captain was waiting to put him ashore under cover of darkness. By the time the launch got up steam again Dreyfus was filled with a sense of ominous foreboding. He no longer expected to find his family or his brother officers waiting to greet him. As he peered anxiously into the gloom of the dark night he released a last faltering hold on his dream of a triumphant return to his homeland; he had come, finally, face to face with the realization that there was more suffering for him ahead, that his nightmare already four and a half years old was not yet over.

The nationalist press had predicted angry protest riots when Dreyfus first set foot on French soil again and government authorities, fearing lest there be some truth in the prophecies, had suppressed all details concerning the prisoner's expected arrival and had ordered that he be returned to France under a heavy veil of secrecy. Accordingly, Dreyfus was brought to a small fishing port during the early hours of the morning of July 1 and was driven from there along a soldier-lined route to a nearby railroad station. A three-hour train ride in the company of three silent, grim-faced guards brought him to another station which he could not remember ever having seen before. From there he was transported by carriage to a military prison which he saw by the first light of the breaking day was in the city of Rennes.

Shortly after his arrival at the Rennes prison Dreyfus was told that he could expect a visit from his wife within a few minutes. Weak and trembling, his nerves stretched to the breaking point, he tried desperately to prepare himself for the joyful encounter he had looked forward to for so long. He was taken to a small, bare room and there he found Lucie. It was no use; he could no longer contain a storm of pent-up emotion. Weeping uncontrollably and unable to utter more than a few stumbling words of love, Alfred Dreyfus embraced his wife while an infantry lieutenant watched impassively.

During the weeks that followed, Dreyfus was allowed to receive further visits from Lucie and to have interviews with his lawyers, Demange and Labori. The attorneys tried to bring him up to date on all that had happened while he was away from France and he pored over the documents and legal transcripts that they brought him. His sufferings, however, had taken a toll on his mental capacities. He could not concentrate for more than short periods of time and no matter what his attorneys told him he seemed utterly unable to comprehend the perfidy of his former superior officers.

Labori and Demange disagreed on the question of how Dreyfus's defense should be conducted. Demange, wanting most of all to get his client acquitted quickly and back to his family, was for sticking close to the question the United Court had left open — did Dreyfus write the bordereau and communicate the information listed in it to enemy agents? Labori, on the other hand, took a larger view. He thought it the mission of the defense not only to defend Dreyfus but also to save France from the abyss of fear and suspicion into which the Dreyfus Affair had plunged her and he therefore favored throwing the brightest possible light on every aspect of the case. Labori finally persuaded Demange to compromise his position. It was agreed that the defense would raise no objections if the prosecution tried to broaden the scope of the trial.

Next, the two lawyers consulted with leading Dreyfusards on how best to guard against a repetition of the angry mob scenes that had sullied Zola's trial. Although the chances of such demonstrations occurring were considerably lessened by the very fact that Dreyfus's second trial would be held outside Paris, it was decided that Zola and Clemenceau, the two men to whom the public was most likely to react violently, should stay away from Rennes during the trial.

16

Trial at Rennes

THE VANGUARD of an army of journalists from every part of the world descended on the small, provincial city of Rennes while the Dreyfus court-martial was still a month away. So many more newspapermen arrived each day in July that before the month was over, Rennes had taken on the air of an occupied city. As the simple tradition-bound Rennois looked on aghast, a horde of men dressed in clothes of unfamiliar cuts and speaking strange-sounding harshly accented French, strode through their once quiet streets, streamed in and out of their Town Hall, asked a thousand questions of everyone they encountered and, when their energy flagged, congregated boisterously in the city's sidewalk cafés.

Having come to cover pre-trial activity in Rennes, the journalists duly filed reports to their editors on the arrangements that had been made for the court-martial: it would begin on August 7; it would be held in the largest room Rennes could boast, the lecture hall of the Lycée, the local high school; and, in deference to the awesome power of the August sun, the hearings would start each day at 6:30 A.M. and end in the early afternoon. This done, the newsmen discovered to their dismay that there was next to nothing else to write about. At the time of Dreyfus's arrival in the

city, stringent police security measures had kept reporters
at such a great distance that no one had been able to catch
more than a glimpse of the back of the prisoner's head as
he was whisked into the military prison; Madame Dreyfus
had appeared in public only briefly before retiring behind
the high garden wall that surrounded the house in which she
had taken lodgings; General Mercier was known to have
arrived in Rennes but he was nowhere to be seen — it was
said that he was comfortably ensconced in a nearby villa
enjoying the lavish hospitality of an old friend, General the
Comte de Saint-Germain; Zola and Clemenceau weren't even
expected. There was, it appeared, no pre-trial activity of
real interest to be found in Rennes. Seemingly unaware of
its reputation as the hottest news spot in the world, the city
slept serenely in the sun. Disgusted, the journalists busied
themselves with sending their papers long, minute descrip-
tions of the outsides of the military prison and the Lycée
and word pictures of the citizens of Rennes — men in blue
blouses and straw hats stolidly towing barges along the
river and women wearing white lace caps kneeling at the
water's edge to do the family wash. And so the month of
July passed in Rennes — the residents of the city staring
openmouthed at their visitors and the sophisticated gentlemen of the world's press staring back, their wonderment at
how men and women could bear such a tedious existence
plain on their faces.

On the morning of August 7, however, Rennes suddenly
came alive. Soon after dawn a covey of important-looking
military officers and a flock of lawyers dressed in long black
gowns and black caps materialized out of nowhere and
converged on the Lycée. Detachments of red-trousered
infantrymen paraded smartly into the streets surrounding

the school building and formed two long lines leading to its entrance. Standing with their feet firmly planted on the ground and their arms outstretched, the soldiers made it clear that they were ready to control any rioting mob that might turn up. But the citizens of Rennes who had gathered outside the Lycée seemed to have no intention of forming a mob; they stood in little knots, well behind the soldiers, placidly gawking at the spendidly uniformed officers and the impressively gowned lawyers.

At the stroke of six there was a sudden bustle of activity as the officers and lawyers, bulging briefcases under their arms, marched purposefully down the avenue formed by the soldiers and into the Lycée. Following closely on their heels, a swarm of newspapermen hurried into the building waving their press passes at the guards as they entered.

At the front of the large, well-lighted lecture hall a raised platform held a long table behind which were chairs for the seven officer-judges of the court-martial. On one side of the room were a small table and chairs for the accused, his guard and his attorneys and on the other side another table and chairs for the prosecuting attorney and his aides. While dozens of witnesses for both sides of the case filed into the rows of seats facing the still empty platform, the journalists were directed to benches and desks set up along the walls. At the very back of the room a small crowd of curious spectators stood behind a line of infantrymen holding fixed bayonets.

A buzz of excited conversation filled the room. Wasn't that General Boisdeffre over there? Indeed, and behind him, Mercier. Picquart looks odd in civilian clothes, does he not? These soldiers are impossibly tall, one cannot see a thing over their shoulders! Look! Over there — Madame Dreyfus! How pale she is! Did no one think to bring a fan? Then, as the seven military judges entered the hall and took their places behind the central table, the talk died out abruptly. All at once everyone in the room was acutely conscious of the drama of the situation; in a moment Alfred Dreyfus would appear before the world for the first time in nearly five years. No more than a shadowy, faceless symbol of treachery to his countrymen when he left France, he had become, in his absence, a figure of world renown. Men in high places had debased their country's ideals in their efforts to keep this man on Devil's Island while other men had sacrificed their careers, had risked their lives, had gone to prison or into exile in their attempts to save him; his name had become a rallying cry or an execration according to the lights of those who uttered it and the pros and cons of his case had been debated in the columns of newspapers all over the world and discussed with passion at dinner tables from San Francisco to Sevastopol. And nobody knew anything about the man himself. What did he look like? What would he say? One part of the audience, expecting a monster, hardened their hearts against him in advance; others, sure of his innocence and remembering the torment he and his family had undergone, felt tears of sympathy spring to their eyes.

"Bring in the prisoner!" The order was barked out by the presiding judge, Colonel Jouast, a small, precise man with a bushy white mustache and a sharply pointed beard. A moment's wait and then, as a door opened and Dreyfus appeared, a chorus of gasps. G. W. Steevens, the correspondent for the English *Daily Mail*, described the man the world was waiting to see:

There came in a little old man — an old, old man
of thirty-nine. A middle-statured, thick-set old man
in the black uniform of the artillery; over the red collar
his hair was gone white as silver, and on the temples
and at the back of the crown he was bald . . . the eyes
under the glasses were set a trifle close together, and
not wholly sympathetic either; you might guess him
hard, stubborn, cunning. But this was only guessing:
what we did see in the face was suffering and effort
— a misery hardly to be borne, and a tense, agonized
striving to bear and to hide it. Here is a man, you
would say, who has endured things unendurable, and
just lives through — maybe to endure more.

Clearly concentrating on every step, Dreyfus walked
forward stiffly. At his chair he stopped, looked toward his
judges, saluted suddenly and, sitting down heavily, removed
his kepi, put it in his lap and folded his white-gloved hands
on top of it. As the audience stared in shocked silence at the
apparition before them, Jouast leaned forward and, in a low
voice, asked the prisoner a question. His answer, only a few
matter-of-fact words, was spoken in loud harsh tones that
grated raspingly on the quiet air. "Alfred Dreyfus, Captain
of Artillery, thirty-nine years old." Dry, hollow, hoarse,
Dreyfus's voice seemed eerily like that of a man who had
died and had been returned to life from the grave.

The business of the court began. A roll call of witnesses.
"Present!" One by one, men famed throughout the world
by virtue of their connection with the accused — ex-Cabinet
Ministers, experts of every variety, generals, colonels, and a
score of lesser officers — stood and answered to their names.
All present but Esterhazy and Du Paty; Esterhazy was still
in hiding in England and Du Paty, the court heard, was too

ill to attend the trial and had doctors' certificates to prove it. After the roll call an hour of tedious preliminary procedure and then Colonel Jouast's attention turned again to the accused. "This document, Captain Dreyfus" — the prisoner was handed a photograph of the bordereau — "is it in your writing?" Dreyfus glanced at the paper in his trembling hand and immediately looked up again, his face twisted in anguish. His mouth opened and for a long moment no sound emerged and then the toneless voice was heard again, high-pitched this time, almost a scream: "I am innocent!"

Time seemed to tumble backward. This white-haired man, his brand-new uniform too big on his wasted flesh, was suddenly once again a sturdy young officer standing on the parade ground of the Ecole Militaire under a wintry sky, protesting his innocence to the general who had degraded him. "I am innocent!" Almost five years had passed; the young officer had grown old on a barren stretch of rock thousands of miles from his homeland; ministries had fallen; great trials had been held; men had been ruined; one man had committed suicide; all because of Alfred Dreyfus and yet, for him nothing had changed. A mistake had been made. He was innocent. That was all he knew. That was all he could say.

At ten o'clock on that first morning of the trial it was announced that the court would next take up the matter of the Army's dossier on Dreyfus and the public was asked to leave the courtroom. The next day a score of foreign newspaper editors protested their correspondents' exclusion from the hearings. Had not the French Army sworn that all its documents relevant to Dreyfus had been delivered to the United Court and had not the United Court made all the Army's material a matter of public record? Why all the secrecy? The truth of the matter was that the Army had requested a closed-doors hearing on its Dreyfus file and the defense had raised no objection. Since there was to be no exclusion of the defense from the proceedings, Demange had insisted on conceding the point to the Army; he thought that an acquittal would be more easily obtained if the Army was given ample opportunity to save its face. It soon appeared, however, that in this instance Demange had miscalculated. It took the court four days to wade through the 600-odd papers that the Army's file now contained and though not one of them could be established as connecting Dreyfus with any illegality, the sense of mystery with which the Army endowed its file left the judges with the vague impression that there were still important state secrets involved in the Dreyfus Case while, in fact, there were none.

On Saturday, June 12, the public was readmitted to the courtroom and the parade of prosecution witnesses began. Now Labori's theory that the broader the scope of the trial the better it would be for Dreyfus and for France came to the test and was found grievously wanting. The Army, given carte blanche to stray from the question of whether or not Dreyfus had written the bordereau, ranged far and wide over all the old familiar ground that had already been assayed by the United Court and pronounced to be barren. Cold, dead issues were warmed over and boldly presented to the judges as living things and their credibility was bolstered by a spate of hearsay evidence which, inadmissible in English and American courts, was acceptable under French law. One Army officer told the court that he had heard Dreyfus called an inveterate gambler and a notorious ladies' man, another testified to having heard someone say that someone else had heard Dreyfus express sympathy for

Germany and a third dragged out the Army-altered text of the Panizzardi telegram, brazenly ignoring the fact that it had been thoroughly discredited by the United Court. In all it was an impressive exhibition of duplicity put on by men whose ambition or fear, or prejudice, or love for the Army they believed threatened, had led them to abandon the truth they had sworn to uphold. And the star of the show was General Mercier.

Slim, straight, impeccably uniformed, Mercier was every inch the general. The very set of his shoulders inspired confidence, his imperious gestures were those of one born to command and his heavy-lidded glance flickered about the courtroom with cool self-assurance. Here, it was clear, was authority and here, too, it soon became apparent to Dreyfusards in the audience, was fanaticism. The worried soldier-politician of 1894 was no more — in his place was a man who had so completely identified his country's interests with his own that he had become an avenging angel — a cold, dispassionate angel, self-righteously intent on destroying a man who he had every reason to believe was innocent of any crime.

Mercier was a fanatic but he was not a madman. Fully aware of the realities of the situation and knowing well that they favored Alfred Dreyfus, he talked around the facts. He addressed the seven military judges as he would a group of subordinates who needed only his clear-headed advice to see the matter before them in its proper light. Seeming to take them into his confidence, he gave them tantalizing glimpses behind the heavy curtain of secrecy with which the Statistical Section veiled its activities; he described a few of the nefarious practices of international espionage agents and some of the unsavory methods forced on those whose business it was to deal with them; he made brief, cryptic references to "one historic night" after Dreyfus's arrest when, while the people of France slept, the nation "teetered on the brink of disastrous war"; he hinted broadly that the German Kaiser took a personal interest in the outcome of the Dreyfus Affair. So devious was the general's strategy and so cunningly was it executed, that without adding anything specific to the court's knowledge of the case, he managed to paint such a black picture of France's position in December, 1894, that any action taken then to save the nation seemed justified. So liberally did Mercier mix truth with half-truth and fact with fiction that he was able to convey a sense of continuing national peril, which peril he made seem to be intimately tied up with the shattered shadow of a man that was Alfred Dreyfus.

Dreyfus had listened in stony-faced silence to the smearing testimony of the first string of prosecution witnesses but his expression had brightened perceptibly when Mercier was called to the stand, and, noting this, Labori and Demange had feared the worst. They had seen that in spite of all they had told him of Mercier's double-dealings, Dreyfus still refused to believe in the general's perfidy; that, incredibly, Dreyfus had emerged from the hell of Devil's Island the same man he had been in 1894 — an acutely rank-snobbish Army officer whose narrow view of the world precluded any serious doubt of the honor and integrity of a general of the Army. As Mercier spoke and the lawyers watched the hope on Dreyfus's face fade into bitter disillusionment, they were afraid that he might not find the strength to bear this cruelest blow of all — inescapable proof that he had in fact been deserted by men in whom he had placed all his trust. For a long time, however, it seemed that Dreyfus would be equal even to this. Then, in the end, Mercier proved too much for him.

Mercier had taken the witness stand at a little before 9 A.M. and it wasn't until the courtroom clock was striking the noon hour that he began to bring his testimony to a close. Then, turning in his chair until he was gazing straight at the prisoner, he said coldly and precisely, "And if I had the least doubt of his guilt, I should be the first to come to Captain Dreyfus and to say to him that I was honestly mistaken." At that an agonized cry split the air. Dreyfus was on his feet, crouched, his fists tightly clenched, his face deathly pale and contorted with fury. "You *should* say that!" he screamed and then moved suddenly as if to spring on his tormenter. The crowd sucked in its breath and a guard quickly put a restraining hand on Dreyfus's arm but Mercier was unperturbed. Pitilessly, he repeated the gist of what he had just said, ". . . I should be the first to make amends for my error." Again a terrible cry, an unearthly shriek wrenched from the depths of a tortured soul — "It is your duty!" But there was no compassion in Mercier and if he felt a sense of duty it was to twist the dagger in his victim's back. Turning to the judges, he continued calmly, "But I say in all conscience that my conviction of his guilt is as firm and unshakeable as ever."

Mercier had scored heavily — there could be no question about that — but Dreyfus's friends remembered that the defense's ace card was still unplayed. They knew that on Monday morning Mercier would have to face Fernand Labori's scathing cross-examination and they were certain that in Labori the general would meet his match. If Mercier was a master of the art of evasion, Labori was equally skilled in circumventing such evasion. Gesturing dramatically, his voice rising and falling, he would probe for the truth until he got it. He would pin the general down and impale him on the spikes of his own misleading insinuations. Ah, yes! One could count on the blond young giant to provide a spectacle worth seeing. On Monday Labori would make Mercier squirm.

But on Monday Labori did not appear in court. Shortly before 6:30, just as the day's proceedings were about to begin, there was a sudden stir at the back of the courtroom and all at once a journalist, wild-eyed and breathing hard, broke through the line of guards, raced to the front of the hall, jumped on a table and at the top of his lungs shouted out a request for a doctor to come to the assistance of a wounded man. A wounded man? Who? How wounded? "Labori — shot!" A stampede of journalists toward the door and then a general exodus as Colonel Jouast hastily announced a temporary adjournment.

Where? In what direction? That way — near the canal! See, there he is! And there was Labori, lying on the ground, his huge bulk sprawled awkwardly, his head in the lap of a young woman, apparently his wife, who bent over him and stroked his hair. A physician pushed through the fast gathering crowd and, kneeling beside the stricken man, made a hasty examination. After a few moments he looked up and announced to the gaping onlookers that it was impossible to tell at once whether or not the wound was serious; there was only a little blood — a good sign, perhaps, but possibly indicative of internal bleeding. A stretcher was summoned and, with his wife and the doctor walking beside him, Labori was carried off to his lodgings.

And the assailant? Vanished! An excited eyewitness to the attack told the police that the man who had fired on Labori had taken to his heels immediately on seeing his victim fall, and that a second man had snatched the lawyer's briefcase and had thereupon taken off after the first. A search was made of the surrounding streets but no trace of the mysterious men could be found. Who were they? It seemed certain to everyone in the crowd that they were professional thugs hired to do away with Labori but there was wide disagreement on the question of who had sent them. Some thought it was Mercier: they said that the general was so afraid of facing Labori's cross-examination that he had tried to get rid of the lawyer. Several others were sure it was the Dreyfus family: had not everyone heard rumors that they were displeased with the line Labori was taking at the trial and was it not well known that Labori was not the man to take orders from anyone, even the family of his client? Even Waldeck-Rousseau's name was mentioned: the Premier, it was said, needed a compromise verdict to keep his Cabinet from falling and it was possible that he had asked Labori to agree to such a verdict, that Labori had refused and that Waldeck-Rousseau had tried to take this way out of his difficulties. The discussion grew more and more heated and the speculation wilder and wilder. It was the Jesuits! No, only the Jewish Syndicate would stoop to murder! No, the Freemasons!

Word that Colonel Jouast had returned to the Lycée broke off the controversy and as the excited crowd hurried back to the courtroom two questions loomed large: would Labori recover from his wound and, if he did, would Jouast adjourn the court-martial procceedings until he was able to return to court? Both were answered before the morning was over. An early bulletin on Labori's condition revealed that the assassin's bullet had lodged in a shoulder muscle and that, since the wound was not serious, Labori would be fit to resume his place in court in a little more than a week. Colonel Jouast, however, declined to wait for Labori. Demange, he said, would have to take over the task of cross-examining the prosecution's witnesses.

Although Demange lacked Labori's fire, he was an exceptionally able lawyer and, of the two defense attorneys, he was the more sophisticated. Labori always strove for dramatic effects but Demange made it a practice to assess the character of the judges or jury he wished to persuade and to act accordingly. Now, keeping firmly in mind that the judges were all army officers, he treated the prosecution's military witnesses with careful consideration. His approach was gentle, his questions polite. Where Labori would have stabbed, he merely prodded; where Labori would have roared, his voice was whisper-soft. Though subtle, his method could be stunningly effective. He asked Jean-Paul Pierre Casimir-Périer, the man who had been President of France at the time when Mercier had said that France was "within measurable distance of war," whether he had slept well on the night that Mercier had called "historic." Casimir-Périer said that he had, that he had been unaware of any unusual danger. When Mercier interrupted to confess that he might have been mistaken about exactly which night it was, Casimir-Périer replied that if there had been any night in that general period of time when the nation was especially threatened he had not known about it. At that, Demange merely looked toward the judges but his raised eyebrow spoke for him. How great could the danger have been, it asked, if General Mercier was hazy about the date and if the President of France had not been informed of its existence? On several other points, however, Demange allowed Mercier and his associates to get clean away; he was acting on his belief that if Dreyfus was to be acquitted the Army must be allowed to preserve a semblance of dignity.

The spectators shifted restlessly in their seats. They had looked forward to watching Labori make lightning flash and thunder roll and Demange had produced no more than a few fitful glimmers of light and a dull counterpoint of charge and denial. The *Daily Mail's* Steevens told of the bewilderment he felt at the time, when he wrote:

> Listening hour by hour, day by day, to testimony such as this finished by quite numbing the judgement. With every fresh witness the cold mist of doubt settled thicker and thicker over the whole affair. I came to Rennes firmly believing Dreyfus innocent; now I no longer knew what I believed. Hour by hour, day by day, the hope of certainty receded further into the shades. It was all a baffling mystery, and a mystery it seemed likely to remain till the day of judgement.

A welcome gust of fresh air blew through the courtroom when Picquart took the stand. The ex-colonel looked drab and dowdy in his civilian clothes — his high, stiff collar was too large for him and his morning coat looked as though it had been made for someone else — but the elegance and strength of his character shone as brightly as ever. Speaking forthrightly, he revealed a broad knowledge of every aspect of the Dreyfus Case and a resolute determination to hew closely to subjects relevant to the questions before the court. Of his long imprisonment for the sake of a man he hardly knew, he said nothing; he clearly considered that to have been an unfortunate but unimportant by-product of the larger struggle in which his country was engaged. He defended Dreyfus's innocence forcefully and with impressive clarity and his strict adherence to the facts contrasted sharply with Mercier's sly evasions.

A dreary succession of prosecution witnesses, each intent on damning Dreyfus, followed Picquart to the stand. Of these, General Boisdeffre seemed the hardest for Dreyfus to take. It was on this kindly-looking, courtly officer that he had pinned his best hopes while he was still on Devil's Island; he had been certain then that it was Boisdeffre who was directing the efforts being made to save him. Now, as Boisdeffre quietly told the judges of his firm belief that Dreyfus and Esterhazy were partners in treason, Dreyfus's mouth twisted in pain. In a moment, however, his face resumed its wooden mask of indifference. Mercier had already trampled on his naïve belief in his superiors' good faith; Boisdeffre could only add a crowning touch to his bitter disillusionment.

The pace of the trial quickened again when Labori returned to court on August 22. The demands of courtesy, and honest sympathy for a man who had suffered pain through no fault of his own, brought both Dreyfusards and anti-Dreyfusards to their feet as the young lawyer, still pale and somewhat weak, entered the courtroom. The judges congratulated him warmly on his recovery and even General Mercier, overcome by his enthusiasm for the amenities of the occasion, came over to the lawyer and shook his hand. But the truce between the two men was short-lived. Labori announced that his mishap had merely postponed his opportunity to fulfill his dearest wish, namely, to have a part in demonstrating the fact of Dreyfus's innocence, and, having thanked the assemblage for their good wishes, he immediately plunged into the business of cross-examining prosecution witnesses and calling others for the defense. It wasn't until two days later, however, that the much heralded confrontation between Labori and Mercier took place.

Wearing the narrow black tunic and red trousers of the infantry, General Mercier took the witness stand and stood with his chin held high, his feet planted a few inches apart and his hands, holding neatly folded white gloves, clasped behind his back. In front of him, Labori paced back and forth, his voluminous black gown flowing from his broad shoulders. By turns gentle and demanding, his voice now conversation-quiet and now strident and insistent, the lawyer stalked his prey. Would M. le Général tell the court about the charges made against Dreyfus in 1894? Did they encompass more than the bordereau itself? They did? There were, then, additional documents involved? Were these documents shown to the other Cabinet Ministers? Only to the Minister of Foreign Affairs? Why was the rest of the cabinet kept in the dark? What date does the War Office attribute to these documents? Ah! then M. le Général is not acquainted with all the details of the case?

Mercier fought back sullenly. Picking and choosing among Labori's questions, he gave direct answers only to those which seemed to pose no threat to his position, bypassed others and flatly refused to answer still others. He implied that patriotic considerations of national security dictated his discretion but, to the disappointment of both Dreyfusards and anti-Dreyfusards, he made no specific references to the now notorious "Kaiser-annotated bordereau." Nationalist editors had been urging him to produce this mysterious "final proof" ever since the beginning of the trial; they understood, they said, the general's reluctance to upset "a delicate balance between peace and war" but they thought that even war was preferable to a further prolongation of the Affair. Dreyfus's supporters, on the other hand, were anxious for the general to bring his pièce de résistance into the open so that it could be examined for authenticity. Mercier, however, made it clear that he was going to keep his superweapon in the never-never land of the "too explosive to reveal." Trapped by Labori into making some damaging admissions, he relied on a new barrage of hints to cover his retreat. Labori laid relentless siege to the general but whenever it seemed that Mercier must at last bow to superior power, he stepped behind the shield he had made of his rank and his knowledge of confidential matters denied to lesser men. When, finally, Labori announced that he had no more questions to put to the witness, only a few of the spectators thought that he had bested his adversary; the others were convinced that Mercier had come out on top.

The prosecution began its mopping-up operations by calling Dreyfus's former military associates to give their opinions of his character and personality. No one of these officers was able to definitely connect Dreyfus with any crime but almost everything they said was unfavorable to the accused and there was an unmistakable ring of sincerity to their statements. Dreyfus had always set everyone's teeth on edge by his priggishness and his vanity, they said. He was unpleasant, humorless, unwilling to make any effort to get along with his fellows, too anxious to get ahead. Although the "normal anti-Semitism" of the French officer caste undoubtedly accounted for some of the adverse comments, even the most dedicated Dreyfusards in the audience saw that more than Dreyfus's Jewishness was involved in his comrades' overwhelming distaste for him.

A "scientific" sideshow wound up the star-studded procession of witnesses. Bertillon, as ebullient as ever, darted about in front of the judges waving charts and graphs as he explained his latest system of handwriting analysis which, he claimed, conclusively proved Dreyfus to be the author of the bordereau. "Five millimeters reticulation!" he crowed happily; "12.5 centimeters gabarit and a millimeter and a quarter imbrication! Always you find it — always — always!" What did his gibberish mean? Simply that on examining those words which appeared twice in the bordereau, Bertillon had found each pair to be almost identical twins, and on examining letters Dreyfus had written before the time of the bordereau, he had found examples of the same peculiarity. Since "no man ever normally writes the same word twice in exactly the same way," Bertillon had concluded that Dreyfus had been in the habit of forging his own handwriting in order to conceal his traitorous activities.

Bertillon's mathematical jargon was impressive but was his method valid? One of the defense's experts thought not. He told the judges that, led by his respect for M. Bertillon's expertise, he had applied M. Bertillon's own system of analysis to several samples of M. Bertillon's own handwriting and had been surprised to find numerous examples of the same peculiarity M. Bertillon had discovered in Dreyfus's letters and in the bordereau. Could it be, he asked, that M. Bertillon, too, was in the habit of forging his own hand and, if so, why?

Finally, it was announced that each side of the case had come to the end of its list of witnesses and that the court would proceed to the hearing of summaries from the prosecuting and defense attorneys. The prosecuting attorney was brief. He pointedly reminded the judges that they would be free of all legal compulsion to explain how they had arrived at their verdict and he urged them to simply weigh the impressions they had received that seemed favorable to the accused against the bulk of those that seemed to condemn him and to vote accordingly. Demange spoke for the defense. Making of his plea an appeal to the judges' humanity, he underlined both the suffering Dreyfus had endured and the accused man's love for his country and he read out loud moving excerpts from letters the prisoner had written from Devil's Island. How, Demange asked the judges, could any man feign the patriotic fervor contained in these words; how could any man have lived through the torment of Devil's Island if he had not been sustained by the hope that his innocence would one day be revealed? Early in the trial Demange's conduct of the defense seemed ponderous and dull; now, as he laid his heart bare to the judges and appealed to theirs, he held his listeners spellbound. As he brought his plea to a close at noon on September 9th, the air was heavy with emotion and one of the judges was seen to wipe tears from his eyes.

After a luncheon recess Dreyfus was asked if there was anything further he wished to say. He rose and in a high, dry monotone announced that he was innocent of any crime and that he was confident that the court-martial judges would save his children's honor. Except for the verdict the trial was over.

At three o'clock the judges retired to a room set aside for their private deliberations and, in accordance with the French custom of removing the accused from the courtroom before the reading of the verdict, Dreyfus was taken to another room. The witnesses and spectators stood up, stretched, moved about and conversed in low voices and on one side of the room the foreign journalists huddled in small groups to discuss the trial and to guess at what the verdict would be.

The foreign newspapermen were almost unanimous in believing Dreyfus innocent and many of them thought an acquittal likely. They said that the judges had struck them as honorable men, men who would be unable to take seriously the mass of opinion and hearsay that the prosecution had presented as evidence of Dreyfus's guilt. Others, maintaining that they saw matters more realistically, took the opposite view. They reminded their colleagues that absence of proof of guilt was no bar to a conviction in France and that the prosecuting attorney had taken pains to assure the judges that the law did not require them to account for their verdict. Besides, the pessimists argued, the judges could not possibly be considering the question of whether or not Dreyfus had written the bordereau since the answer to that was buried beneath an immovable weight of contradictory evidence; they must, instead, be addressing themselves to the question Mercier had posed: who shall be called guilty — a single Jew or the whole French Army with which the French people identified themselves, or, to put it more succinctly, who was guilty — Dreyfus or Mercier? But some of the journalists stubbornly continued to hope for the best. The judges, they said, could not help but be aware that all of Europe was looking to them for a just decision and, realizing that they had it within their power to redeem France's shamed name, they would certainly acquit.

When an hour had passed and the judges had still not returned, it began to look as though the optimists could be right. The judges at Dreyfus's first court-martial had taken only a few minutes to reach their verdict; Zola's jury was out only a little more than a half hour. This time it was clear that the judges were disagreeing and that was a good sign for Dreyfus. If more than two of them voted to acquit, Dreyfus would have to be set free.

It was hot in the courtroom and as the afternoon wore on the temperature climbed unmercifully. The spectators, perspiring and restless, kept their eyes glued on the door to the judges' chamber. It wasn't until five o'clock that it opened. Then a call rang out: *Présentez armes!* There was a rattle of rifles and a shuffle of people rising to their feet and then tense silence as the judges filed into the courtroom and took their places at the central table. When the audience had resumed their seats, Colonel Jouast stood and, in a voice shaking with emotion, announced the verdict: "In the name of the French people . . . By five votes to two, guilty . . . guilty with extenuating circumstances . . . punishment: ten years imprisonment."

Labori and Demange stood with their heads bowed and tears streamed down the older lawyer's cheeks. After a moment, Labori whispered a few words to Demange and when Demange shook his head, Labori walked slowly out of the courtroom toward the room where Dreyfus was waiting. Later Labori told reporters that on hearing the verdict Dreyfus said only, "Console my wife."

Rennes received the news of the verdict with apparent unconcern. Leaving the Lycée, foreign journalists were shocked to note that there were no more than the usual number of people in the surrounding streets. The trial of the century was over, tragically over, and there were no demonstrations, no outbursts of indignation — nothing; just the people of Rennes going about their business as usual. Outraged, G. W. Steevens wrote:

> "In the name of the French people!" The first beginning of natural life again was a dull, hot, unreasonable rancour against the French people — against calm Rennes — against the honest troopers at their horses' bridles — the army — the judges — anybody. Reason had whispered for weeks that you must allow for prejudice, for prepossessions honestly and even creditably come by and difficult to shake off, for the delicacies of the judges' positions, for the suspicious mysteries of the case . . . There was every reason why it should be so — and it was so, and we were bitterly angry. The band was playing in the cafe, I remember, as I passed — the usual band that amuses us every evening; what an outrage!
>
> Rennes was calm. Men were tugging barges up the river, and women were washing clothes — just as they had yesterday before this portent fell . . . It was monstrous. This monstrous wrong was done: a man whom most believe innocent, whom none can prove guilty, was coolly, deliberately, solemnly condemned and condemned for the second time. And Rennes was calm — my God! Better that they had torn him to pieces with their hands.

17

And Still The Affair

TEN DAYS after his second conviction for the crime of treason Dreyfus was a free man. The rider attached to the Rennes verdict, "with extenuating circumstances," allowed Loubet to offer Dreyfus a presidential pardon and although Dreyfus said at first that he would not accept it, that he wanted not mercy but justice, he finally did so. Lucie's tearful pleas had persuaded him to take advantage of the opportunity offered him to repair his shattered health before pressing on with the fight to clear his name. There could be no doubt that he needed a period of recuperation. He still suffered frequent attacks of the fever that had plagued him on Devil's Island, his sleep was still broken each night by recurrent nightmares, he was still racked with rheumatic pains and he was not yet able to concentrate on any mental effort for a sustained period of time. He made a bargain with the government. He would withdraw the appeal for an Army review of the Rennes verdict that he had already filed and he would accept the pardon if it was clearly understood that he reserved the right to try to prove his innocence at some future date.

When Clemenceau heard that Dreyfus was about to accept a pardon he was furious. The Dreyfusard cause had suffered a reverse, yes, but it must be carried forward at once against all odds. Dreyfus must appeal, must fight for a new trial and, if at that new trial he was convicted again, he must appeal again, and again, if necessary, until at last an impartial jury was found to clear him. The overriding question, Clemenceau thundered, was no longer that of one man wrongly convicted but of France herself, disastrously shamed by the denial of justice to that man. Mathieu argued with him. He told Clemenceau that his brother could not possibly survive a second sentence and he reminded him that a loving family had already been separated for almost five years and that two little children who could not remember their father's face still thought that he was on foreign military service. Clemenceau softened. Grudgingly he admitted to Mathieu, "If I were your brother, I should accept the pardon." Other militant Dreyfusards were less compassionate. Their homes had been stoned by anti-Semitic rioters and they had walked the streets of Paris at the peril of their lives and now as they saw the man for whom they had sacrificed so much apparently withdraw from the battle, they were disappointed and angry. Charles Péguy spoke for them when he said bitterly, "We might have died for Dreyfus; Dreyfus has not died for Dreyfus."

With the pardon peace descended on France. The problems of the Dreyfus Affair seemed to have been neatly disposed of; the court-martial verdict had preserved the honor of the Army and now, for those troubled by the thought of a possibly innocent man convicted for the second time, there was the comforting knowledge that that man was at liberty and reunited with his family. Most Frenchmen concluded that a satisfactory best had been made out of a most difficult and unpleasant situation and, by now thoroughly bored with the whole Dreyfus Affair, they proceeded to dismiss it from their thoughts. There were other, pleasanter things to think about. For one thing, there was the Paris Exposition, due to open in April, which, now that the Dreyfus Case seemed to be closed, could be made into a smashing commercial success.

While Frenchmen settled back to enjoy the peace and quiet so long denied them by the Affair, the rest of the world fulminated in angry indignation. Guilty with extenuating circumstances! How ridiculous! A presidential pardon for a twice-convicted traitor? Grotesque! Reason dictates that if a man is guilty of treason he must be punished and that if he is innocent he must be acquitted. How transparent the French were! Unable to prove Dreyfus's guilt and yet wishing him to be guilty, they had come up with this impossible verdict and irrational pardon. Almost everywhere outside of France people saw the Rennes verdict as a slap in the face of justice. Anti-French demonstrations were staged in European and American cities; tricolors were publicly burned and French embassies were stoned. Foreign newspapers urged their readers to refrain from buying French export products and to boycott the Paris Exposition. Frenchmen, however, shrugged off the criticism directed at their country. The incident, they said, is closed.

But was it? Premier Waldeck-Rousseau knew that it was not and he suspected that it never would be until Dreyfus's innocence was finally established. Nevertheless, he welcomed the period of public calm that followed the pardon. He needed a respite from constant political dissension in order to carry out a series of reforms he had planned. These reforms, he told his close associates, would not only invigorate the Republic but would also lead to a final and satisfactory end to the Affair by correcting the conditions that had produced it in the first place. What were those conditions? According to Waldeck-Rousseau they were the existence of dangerous pockets of anti-Republic power within the Army and an imperfect separation of Church and State.

One after the other, the Statistical Section, the Army classification committee responsible for promotions to the rank of general, and the Assumptionist and Jesuit orders felt the effects of Waldeck-Rousseau's reforming zeal. The highly secret nature of the Statistical Section's work had allowed it extraordinary freedom from government interference and under Colonel Henry's influence its officer staff had become more and more outspokenly anti-Republic; now the Section was peremptorily relieved of its counterespionage duties which were handed over to the Sureté, the civilian police investigatory agency. Next, an official ax was taken to the élite group of Army officers who routinely winnowed out all but aristocratic, Church-influenced, anti-Republic and anti-Semitic candidates for the rank of general; they were stripped of their power and the duties they had performed were assigned to the Minister of War. Then, moving against the political power of the most intransigent clerical interests, the government raided the offices of the bitterly anti-Semitic Assumptionist newspaper, *La Croix*. An enormous sum of money, clearly intended to finance the Assumptionists' campaign against the Republic, was seized and an official investigation of the order's activities was set in motion. As a final step in the first stage of his plan to strengthen the Republic, Waldeck-Rousseau obtained parliamentary approval for a bill which made three years in a state school a prerequisite for public service and had the effect of taking the education of future Army officers out of the hands of the Jesuit priests.

But, while the Premier was chopping away at the roots of the Affair, its malodorous flower, the twice-over conviction

of an innocent man, still bloomed and a group of die-hard
Dreyfusards, declaring themselves unable to stand the stench,
tried to arouse parliamentary interest in securing a new
trial for Dreyfus. Waldeck-Rousseau moved to stop them;
he feared that a renewal of public agitation would unseat
him before he could carry out all his plans to pump new vigor
into the Republic. He quickly proposed to Parliament an
amnesty bill to cover everyone involved in the Affair except
Dreyfus himself (Dreyfus had made his right to continue
the struggle to clear his name a condition of his acceptance
of Loubet's pardon).

An amnesty! An official act of "forgiving and forgetting"
to apply to innocent and guilty alike! No! cried the Dreyfusards, the bill must not be passed! An amnesty might well
accomplish the Premier's purpose of maintaining the false
peace that had soothed France since the pardon, but it would,
at the same time, heap new injustices on the old. For one
thing, it would relieve General Mercier of ever having to
answer to Parliament for his illegal acts of 1894; for another,
it would deprive innocent men of their chance to prove their
innocence. Although Dreyfus was specifically excluded from
the provisions of the bill, the amnesty, if passed, would strike
him a devastating blow; by putting an end to all pending
lawsuits connected with the Affair it would dry up his most
promising sources for the "new facts" he would have to
have before he could file an appeal for a new trial. Other
innocent men caught up in the toils of the Affair would be
equally hard-hit by an amnesty. Zola, still charged with having insulted the Army in "J'Accuse," would be unable to
disprove the charge; the suit brought by Henry's widow
against Reinach for "defaming" the colonel's memory would
grind to a halt and leave Reinach in the position of a man

who had been attacked and whose sole weapon of defense
had been taken away from him; Picquart, discharged from
the Army under a cloud of suspicion, would be unable to dis-
pel that cloud. Hoping to counter at least some of the
Dreyfusard objections to the bill, Waldeck-Rousseau's Minister of War, General Galliffet, offered to reinstate Picquart
into the Army without further ado. Picquart proudly refused
the offer; he announced that he would not even consider
re-entering the Army through a back door. Writing to the
Premier, he said:

> It is inadmissible that this situation be prolonged,
> and that I indefinitely stand without judgement. I
> demand to be judged. I demand that I be permitted
> to show publicly that the accusations against me are
> based on fraud and lies . . . The law of amnesty
> would hit me twice over; it would give me amnesty
> for a felony that I have not committed and it would
> include me in one and the same measure with General
> Mercier and his associates.

Even the nationalists railed against the bill. Pretending
to be unaware of the great boon that an amnesty would be
to the generals — to Gonse, Boisdeffre and Billot as well as
to Mercier — the Army-inspired press insisted that the
"criminal" Picquart and Reinach had pressured the Premier
into proposing the bill in order to save themselves.

In spite of all the vociferous objections to his bill, the Premier refused to withdraw it. As a longtime politician he
knew that time had a way of quieting even the loudest out-
cries and he was confident that if Parliament refused to pass
the amnesty at once it would do so after a few months' time.
Privately, the Premier conceded that his amnesty would not

serve the cause of justice. Nevertheless, he sincerely believed that in proposing the bill he had done the best he could for France.

For France! How many times since 1894 those two stirring words had been used to cover up the snowballing injustices of the Dreyfus Affair. General Mercier had engineered Dreyfus's original conviction "for France"; Gonse and Boisdeffre had sought to silence Picquart "for France", Billot had rigged Esterhazy's court-martial "for France"; Zola's jury had been convinced to vote guilty "for France." Colonel Henry, found out by General Cavaignac, had insisted that he had forged "for France." "For France" Frenchmen had consented to a campaign of systematic slander and violence against their Jewish countrymen and at Rennes a court-martial jury had struck a bargain with its conscience by returning the non sequitur verdict of "guilty with extenuating circumstances" — again "for France." Why had a "guilty" man been pardoned and why did the Premier now propose an all-encompassing amnesty? For France! And still the Dreyfus Affair festered in France's soul.

Clemenceau turned out column after column of warnings to his countrymen. France is sick, he shouted, and only the truth can cure her. But only a handful of Frenchmen listened to him. Crowds were flocking to the Paris Exposition and the reassuring jingle of coins in their money boxes convinced the people of France that there was no pressing need to take the bitter medicine Clemenceau prescribed.

And how had Dreyfus reacted to the amnesty bill? He had protested it but, thought Labori and Picquart, not loudly or often enough. Alfred Dreyfus at close range had proven to be considerably less than the man his supporters had imagined him to be while he was still on Devil's Island. How

noble his courage and his determination to clear his name
had seemed then! As a voiceless prisoner chained to a distant rocky island he had been a perfect symbol of the battle
being waged in France in his name. The man who sat in the
prisoner's chair at Rennes, however, seemed singularly ill-
suited for the heroic role that had been thrust on him. True,
he had triumphantly managed to survive an unimaginable
ordeal — but for what? Apparently for the sake of his precious name alone. At Rennes he gave no indication of any
sustained interest in the larger issues involved in his case and
he showed no more than a perfunctory concern for the effect
of the trial on anyone but himself. Indeed, his narrow out-
look, his preoccupation with his own misfortunes and his
cringing respect for the insignia of rank, even when that
insignia was worn by men who had betrayed him, seemed
to many to mark him as a man cast in a mold very like that
which had formed his betrayers. At Rennes, one disillusioned
Dreyfusard had remarked, "If Dreyfus's name had not been
Dreyfus, he would undoubtedly have been an anti-Dreyfusard." Many years later, Clemenceau was to say of Dreyfus,
"He was the only one who understood nothing of the Affair;
he stood abysmally below it."

For many, disenchantment with Dreyfus began on the day
when Picquart was first called to the witness stand at Rennes.
Expecting a dramatic and poignant scene when the prisoner
came face to face with the man who had sacrificed so much
for him, they were sadly disappointed. So was Picquart. He
had not wanted thanks but he had hoped to see some sign
that Dreyfus understood how dearly bought his return from
Devil's Island had been. He saw none. Dreyfus had merely
looked at Picquart coolly and his stony expression had
remained unchanged the whole time that Picquart was on

the stand. Was it, as some said, a matter of Dreyfus's being so intent on obtaining an acquittal on the basis of his innocence alone that he refused to indulge in any display of emotion that might possibly play on the judges' sympathies? Or were others, less kind, right when they said that Dreyfus was so caste-snobbish that he considered it unnecessary to react in one way or another to the undistinguished looking man in his ill-fitting civilian clothes? It was impossible to know for certain but from that time on, Picquart began to think less and less of Dreyfus and more and more of himself. With the presidential pardon, his growing resentment of Dreyfus's attitude had hardened into bitterness; Dreyfus had accepted the pardon without first consulting Picquart. Of course, Picquart said to his friends, Dreyfus's intense desire to be reunited with his family was entirely natural, but did he not recognize that in accepting the pardon he tacitly acknowledged not only his own guilt but that of Picquart as well?

Dreyfus went from Rennes to his sister's home in Carpentras in the south of France and from there he wrote to Picquart asking to see him that he might tell him in person of the tremendous gratitude he felt. Perhaps Picquart thought Dreyfus's friendly advance had been offered too late; he did not reply to Dreyfus's letter.

On December 2, 1899, soon after Waldeck-Rousseau proposed his amnesty bill, Dreyfus wrote a letter protesting it to the government and in March, 1900, he followed up his first protest with another. Then, a month later, he took his family to live on the shores of Lake Geneva in Switzerland "on the advice of physicians" and nothing more was heard from him. Word reached France that he was making excellent progress in regaining his health and was basking in the warmth of the thousands of letters he had received from all

over the world congratulating him on his freedom. Back in
France Picquart told Labori that he thought it quite possible
that Dreyfus had made a deal with Waldeck-Rousseau — his
freedom in return for his silence and his absence from France.

Labori was already embittered against Dreyfus, and
against his family as well. When the trial at Rennes was
drawing to a close, Mathieu and Lucie Dreyfus had insisted
that Demange undertake the summation of the case for the
defense. Quite correctly, they believed that of the two lawyers Demange was the more deeply concerned with his
client's immediate interests; it seemed to them that Labori
was far too idealistic, too anxious to resolve the whole com-
plex struggle between the democratic and authoritarian sides
of France at a time when it was his duty to concentrate on
getting Dreyfus acquitted. Labori was miffed at having to
step aside just when the most dramatic trial of his career
was reaching its climax. Dreyfus's decision to accept the
pardon had sharpened his annoyance and when he saw the
proposed amnesty threaten to quench all his high hopes of
bringing the Dreyfus Affair to a stunning crescendo of justice
he grew angry. He agreed with Picquart that Dreyfus's long
silence, coupled with his continued absence from France,
seemed to imply a willingness to accept the pardon as a final
solution of his case.

Rumors to the effect that he was remaining abroad "at the
request of the French government" reached Dreyfus during
the autumn of 1900 and he hurried back to Paris to scotch
them. He stayed only long enough to demonstrate that he
was at liberty to go wherever he chose and then returned to
Switzerland to complete his convalescence. In October, 1901,
his health finally restored, he brought his family back to
Paris to stay. In the meantime, while the fate of the amnesty

bill hung in the balance, the rift in the Dreyfusard ranks had widened.

On the one side were Clemenceau, Zola, Labori and Picquart. They believed that in proposing the amnesty bill Waldeck-Rousseau had compromised the cause of justice and that Dreyfus, in remaining largely outside the fight to defeat the bill, had deserted it. They wanted Dreyfus to plunge back into battle to clear his name even though an immediate renewal of the struggle promised little hope of success; they were convinced that the fight had to be carried forward regardless of consequences lest Frenchmen forget that there ever was such a thing as the Dreyfus Affair. The prolongation of the Affair had changed these Dreyfusards' objectives. Once each was preoccupied with the idea of simple justice for Dreyfus; now Picquart was more interested in his own vindication and Clemenceau, Labori and Zola frankly aimed at the decisive defeat of the militarist, clerical and autocratic forces that seemed to them to be choking the Republic.

In the other Dreyfusard camp were Mathieu Dreyfus, Demange, Reinach and Mornard, Lucie Dreyfus's attorney during the United Court of Appeals hearings. These men, reluctant to subject Dreyfus to another round of fruitless trials and hearings, believed it best to wait until the necessary "new facts" were found before precipitating a new crisis. Clemenceau raged against the advocates of patience. To Reinach he roared, "You sacrifice the claims of all suppressed people to a private interest." Reinach, in turn, accused Clemenceau: "You make out of a living creature a battering ram against military and political institutions."

In December of 1900 Parliament passed the amnesty bill into law and, as a thick fog of legal oblivion started to settle over the Dreyfus Affair, Zola and Clemenceau despaired of

ever again finding a clear path to justice. Mathieu Dreyfus
was more optimistic. He told his brother that if he could not
find proof of his innocence in the courts he would find it
someplace else. Doggedly, Mathieu followed every lead, no
matter how lukewarm or unpromising, and when one trail
led only to a blind alley, he cheerfully looked around for
another. Hearing of Mathieu's efforts, Labori scoffed. "He
will get nowhere," the lawyer told Clemenceau and Zola,
"the amnesty has put France to sleep. Once the mention of
Dreyfus's name was enough to set off a riot; now he walks
the streets of Paris unnoticed."

Labori was right. France seized on the amnesty as a welcome excuse to resist all attempts to reopen the Dreyfus Case.
Wherever Mathieu turned in his efforts to uncover evidence
that could establish his brother's innocence he ran into a wall
of unyielding resistance. What does it matter, after all, he
was asked, whether or not your brother is officially cleared?
His troubles are over now, are they not? Since France is at
last at peace is it not best to let the matter rest? Within a
few months all talk of the Affair dried up; newspapers that
once had clamored for Dreyfus's blood ignored him; the
Dreyfus Affair, France assured the world, is over.

And yet, paradoxically, it was while Frenchmen were doing
their best to forget Alfred Dreyfus that the effects his case
had had on France first became clearly discernible. A wave of
anti-militarism gradually spread through the country as the
French people, dismayed and disillusioned by Dreyfusard
exposures of the generals' follies and duplicities, turned
against the Army they had loved so intemperately only a
short time before. Revolted by the anti-Semitic excesses of
the Affair, most Frenchmen stopped listening to the apostles

of hatred in their midst. Shocked by the shameful part clerical interests had played in the campaign to hide the truth,
the public began to display an increasing willingness to
accept government efforts to strip the French Church of its
remaining influence over the nation's temporal life. Nevertheless, although their long-held prejudices had been shaken
and their attitudes toward cherished institutions had been
profoundly altered by the Dreyfus Affair, the French people
continued to turn their backs on Alfred Dreyfus.

It wasn't until two years after the passing of the amnesty
law that Dreyfus came to France's attention again. Then, a
sudden, tragic stroke of fate put him back for a brief stay in
the headlines of the French press.

18

Climax and Anticlimax

ZOLA DEAD. CHIEF OF PARIS POLICE BIDS DREYFUS STAY AWAY
FROM FUNERAL. On September 28, 1902, Emile Zola had come
with his wife from their country home in Medan to spend
the winter in their Paris apartment. Although the summer
was barely over there was already a wintry chill in the air;
Zola lit the coal stove that heated the apartment and; on retiring that first night back in Paris, the Zolas kept the windows
of their bedroom tightly shut. While they slept the stove,
newly and imperfectly repaired, gave off clouds of carbon
monoxide gas and both Zola and Madame Zola sickened during the night. The next morning, their maid, alarmed by
how late the Zolas seemed to be sleeping, knocked on their
door and, getting no answer, entered the bedroom and found
Madame Zola on the bed, barely alive, and Zola lying
stretched out on the floor, already dead.

Everywhere people mourned the loss of a towering literary
figure and foreign newspaper editorials paid glowing tributes
to the courage Zola had shown in publishing "J'Accuse" at a
time when to do so was to risk fame, fortune and even life
itself. In Zola's own country, however, Clemenceau's was one
of the few voices that spoke out in praise of Zola's selfless
service to France. In a speech before the senate the grieving
Clemenceau said:

There have always been people strong enough to
resist the most powerful kings, to refuse to bow before
them; [but] there have been very few to resist the
masses, to stand up alone to the misled multitude
. . . To Zola goes the glory of having given the signal
to that peaceful revolt of the spirit which in our tormented France was nothing less than a revolution
through the medium of thought.

Zola's death raised a frightening question in the mind of
the chief of the Paris police. Would the funeral of the author
of "J'Accuse" revive old passions and send a mob raging
again through the streets of the city? Fearing that if Dreyfus were present it might, the chief warned Dreyfus of the
possibility of "unpleasant incidents" and asked him to stay
away. Dreyfus refused the request. He told the chief that
he personally feared nothing and that he considered it a
compelling duty to be present when Zola was laid to rest.

Madame Zola, too, was worried. She had recovered from
the sickening effects of the coal gas in time to attend to the
sad task of arranging her husband's funeral and, anxious lest
the dignity of the occasion be impaired by a renewal of the
violent controversy that had once swirled around Zola, she,
too, begged Dreyfus to stay away. She went even further.
Inviting Anatole France to deliver the funeral oration, she
asked him to avoid all mention of the Affair in his remarks
and to confine his praise of Zola to his literary achievements.
Dreyfus had refused the police chief's request but he felt duty
bound to respect Madame Zola's wishes and he gave her his
promise to do as she asked. Not so Anatole France. The
novelist politely informed the bereaved woman that if she insisted on limiting what he could say in his eulogy he would be

unable to accept the honor she offered him. Because Anatole France now held her dead husband's place as France's leading literary light, Madame Zola was determined to have him and no other deliver the oration and she answered him by saying that she would rely on his tact. But France was not interested in being tactful about Zola and he telegraphed the widow: "Under these circumstances it is impossible for me to speak at Zola's grave." Madame Zola gave in. France's insistence on memorializing her husband's courage must have strengthened her own; she wired the novelist giving him complete liberty to say what he chose and she sent a message to Dreyfus saying that she had withdrawn her request for him to absent himself from the funeral.

Anatole France did not mince words at the burial services. Addressing the assembled mourners, he said:

> With the calm and solemnity that a place of death commands, I am going to remind you of the dark days when the government was in the grip of egotism and fear. Some people began to recognize the injustice done but it was supported and defended by so many open and secret powers that even the boldest hesitated. Those whose duty it was to speak up kept silent . . . Those who did not fear for themselves were fearful of exposing their party to incalculable dangers. The masses, misled by dreadful lies, excited by monstrous aspersions, felt betrayed . . .
>
> The darkness became more impenetrable. Uneasy silence ruled. This was the moment when Zola wrote to the President of the Republic that poised and frightful letter which unmasked fraud and forgery . . .
>
> In those days, heavy with crime, good citizens despaired of the fate of the country, the moral destiny of France . . . Justice, honor, spirit — all seemed lost.

All was saved. Zola discovered not merely a miscarriage of justice. He exposed the conspiracy of all the forces of violence and suppression that had joined hands to kill social justice, the idea of the Republic and the free spirit of France . . .

France is the country of reason and of the pondering spirit, the country of just judges and humane philosophers . . . Zola deserved well of France when he refused to accept the fact that justice was no more in France.

Do not pity him for what he had to endure and suffer. Envy him! He had deserved well of the country, as he had of the world by an immense lifework and a great act. Fate and his courage swept him to the summit; to be, for one instant, the conscience of mankind.

Madame Zola and the police chief had worried for nothing; in spite of Dreyfus's presence there were no incidents of any kind to mar the quiet solemnity of the funeral services. The white-hot flame of fury that Zola had once ignited in the hearts of so many of his countrymen had apparently burned down, flickered and, finally, gone out. Zola was dead and as far as the people of Paris were concerned he could rest in peace. The streets of the city were quiet as his mourners left the cemetery and drove home in their carriages.

Zola was dead and it seemed to most Dreyfusards that all hope of ever bringing about the clear-cut triumph of justice that Zola had wanted so badly for his country was also dead. Restrained by the amnesty's legal straitjacket, Picquart and Reinach could do nothing, and although it was open to Dreyfus to appeal for a new trial, he had first to find fresh evidence to present to the courts and he had not yet uncovered any.

Still, Mathieu Dreyfus was not ready to give up. There was still the possibility that the puzzle of the "Kaiser-annotated bordereau" could be run to earth. Mathieu knew that if this mysterious document existed at all it was a forgery, but he remembered that the famous "Henry forgery" had been used against his brother to excellent effect at his first court-martial and he had recently found reason to believe that this much discussed but never publicly revealed "annotated bordereau" had secretly been shown to the judges at Rennes. If what Mathieu suspected was true, it would go far toward explaining how supposedly honorable men had found it possible to recondemn a man whose guilt had not been proven in court. Moreover, proof that the judges had seen a document that had not been shown to the defense would constitute a more than adequate "new fact." Acting on his hunch, Mathieu made discreet approaches to the judges involved but, it turned out, to no avail. The judges would not discuss the matter. Discouraged finally, Mathieu abandoned his independent search. He conferred with his brother and told him of his conviction that the "new facts" they needed lay hidden in the War Office files. In November the Dreyfus brothers came to the conclusion that they must somehow arouse Parliament's interest in ordering an official re-examination of those files.

The Dreyfuses had set themselves a formidable task; the overwhelming majority of Deputies and Senators would be sure to oppose any attempt to reopen the Dreyfus case — those on the Right would be unwilling to place the Army's honor in jeopardy again and those on the Left would fear that a new surge of public agitation might obstruct the government's plans to disarm its nationalist foes. How then to spark a new review of the case? Should Alfred make a formal request for a government investigation? If he did, might not Parliament simply brush it off?

Months of consultations among leading Dreyfusards produced a plan. The Socialist Deputy, Jean Juarès, would use a scheduled Chamber debate on an almost wholly unrelated matter as a springboard for bringing the sinister mystery of the "annotated bordereau" to the attention of the Chamber. The hope was that in so doing he would pique enough interest in the subject to ensure a favorable reaction to a request for an investigation which Dreyfus would then file with the government. The plan was put into action in April 1903 and although Juarès failed to achieve all its objectives his speech in the Chamber did provoke a promise from General André, the new Minister of War, to conduct a "personal investigation" of the War Office files on the Dreyfus Case.

Political wrangling over the proposed investigation kept André from fulfilling his promise until the summer of 1903 but, once started, his inquiry produced startling results almost at once. Official reports favorable to Dreyfus and secretly suppressed by the Statistical Section suddenly came to light; an important document, widely assumed to have been delivered by Dreyfus to the Germans, was found among the papers of a recently deceased French officer; and it was discovered that Colonel Henry had altered at least one more of the vital documents in the case. A careful search of the Army files had turned up an official copy of the Madame Bastian–obtained note from the Italian military attaché, Panizzardi, to his German counterpart, von Schwartzkoppen, and this copy revealed that the Italian had told the German that a certain "P," not "D," had brought him "many interesting things." André submitted a report on his findings to the

Ministry of Justice in October and recommended that the proper steps be taken to ensure that "the truth may finally emerge." The Minister of Justice sent André's report to the Court of Criminal Appeals with a request for a ruling on the admissibility of an appeal of the Rennes verdict.

Once again a procession of the leading characters in the Dreyfus Affair filed before the justices of the Criminal Court. Time had stooped the proud military posture of some and had whitened the hair and wrinkled the brows of others but the five and a half years that had passed since the court had first considered the Dreyfus Case had not changed the testimony of the Army's witnesses a whit — Dreyfus was guilty; the Army had overwhelming proofs of his guilt; those who said he was innocent were seeking to destroy the Army and bolster the strength of France's enemies. It was all drearily familiar, a tedious re-run of old lies and threadbare evasions. Madame Bastian, the onetime cleaning woman–spy made a brief appearance in the witness box and startled the assemblage in the courtroom by spitting out a stream of uncouth anti-Semitic abuse. The Germans, it appeared, had discovered her duplicity and had turned her out of their employ; the French Statistical Section, finding her usefulness to them at an end, had promptly followed suit. Old now, and more than a little mad, Madame Bastian made it abundantly clear that she blamed "the Jews" for all her troubles.

Three of France's most eminent scientists, men of unassailable integrity, gave a report to the court on a careful examination they had made of Bertillon's various systems of handwriting analysis. Their report was devastating. It branded the eccentric little man's methods as "unscientific," "prejudiced" and, most cutting of all, "ridiculous." Seeing

Bertillon's support for the Army's case finally demolished, the judges turned to the matter of the "annotated bordereau." But no one, not even General Mercier, would swear to ever having seen either its original or a copy. Pinned down, Mercier mumbled that although he had not actually seen the document he had heard about it in great detail from an officer he considered "thoroughly reliable." When Mercier's informant, an elderly colonel, was called to the stand, it turned out that he had not seen the document either but had heard of it from someone whom, he said, he was not at liberty to name. That did it. The judges made it plain that it would be impossible for them to give further serious attention to a document the very existence of which remained in doubt.

By mid-November there seemed to be no substance left to the Army's case for Dreyfus's guilt; on the other hand, there was a mass of new evidence pointing to his innocence. On November 28 the Court of Criminal Appeals ruled that Dreyfus was entitled to a new trial and sent his case once again to the United Court of Appeals.

Now that the end was in sight Dreyfus could hardly contain his impatience. Nine years had passed since that terrible morning when, all unwitting, he had reported to Major Du Paty de Clam at the Ministry of War to hear the Major accuse him of the infamy of treason. Nine years — five of them spent in the torment of Devil's Island! Nine years of shame and dishonor! All through those long years Dreyfus had waited, proud and stoical and, many said, supremely selfish, his eyes glued on the single objective of his vindication. While his country had writhed under the vicious attacks of counterrevolutionary forces his case had brought into the open, he had had only one thought, had said essentially only one thing — "I am innocent!" — over and over again — "I am innocent!" Some of his countrymen — at first just a few and then thousands of others — had rallied to his side. Convinced of his innocence and awakened to the grave threat to their national ideals inherent in his conviction, they had imbued his anguished cry with other and deeper meanings. According to their lights, they had heard in it a summons to save the Army from disgrace, a desperate plea to rescue French democracy from the clutches of resurgent authoritarianism, a call to defend the civilian rule of law against a power hungry Army and clergy. Brave men, dedicated sons of the Great Revolution, they had made Dreyfus's cause their own and that of France herself. But for Dreyfus, the battlefield never enlarged. While in the streets, in the press, in Parliament and in the courts, the Revolution raged again, he lived, suffered, endured for one purpose only — to redeem his honor, to clear his children's name.

How mercilessly those nine years had treated him! Delivered at last from the all but insupportable physical and spiritual deprivation of Devil's Island, he had returned to his homeland only to feel the fierce sting of his countrymen's hatred and later, after the pardon and the amnesty, the even crueller pain of their indifference. Almost as hard to bear had been the harsh sound of bitter wrangling among his friends, the ugly spectacle of brave, good men turning against each other in disillusionment, suspicion and misunderstanding. Days, weeks, months, years. How slowly the time had passed! But now, miraculously, all at once there was reason again to hope. Having waited so long, Dreyfus found it excruciatingly difficult to wait any longer.

Characteristically shortsighted, Dreyfus saw in the Criminal Court's ruling for a new trial no more than thrilling reason to believe that his longed-for vindication might yet become

a reality, but a handful of thoughtful Frenchmen recognized
that it implied considerably more than that — that it was
actually a manifesto of hope not just for one man cruelly
wronged but for a whole people whose future as a democratic
nation had become inextricably intertwined with the fate of
that man. They saw that in insisting on a reopening of the
Dreyfus Case, the Criminal Court had issued a stern reminder
to all Frenchmen that while they were governed by the
rule of law they could not afford to pay the price of an
individual's rights for the prize of a calm and ordered society.

The public reacted neither one way nor another to the
court's ruling. They were bored with Alfred Dreyfus. Thrilling tales of espionage, international conspiracy and corruption in high places had once riveted their attention on the
Affair but when, after Rennes, its excitement index had
plunged, so had their interest in its final outcome. Nineteen
months were to pass between the Criminal Court's ruling for
a new trial and the beginning of that trial and Alfred Dreyfus chafed at the delay. Not so the French people. Their
vision blurred by the myriad details of their daily lives, they
could not see the real significance of the Dreyfus Affair and
it mattered not at all to them whether or not its final scene
was ever acted out.

Why did it take the French courts so long to implement the
Criminal Court's decision? It seems likely that the explanation lay in large part in the single-minded determination of
the new Premier, Emil Combes, to bring about a final separation of Church and State. Combes, a man of strong anti-
clerical sentiments, had succeeded Waldeck-Rousseau in 1902
and it is more than probable that he did whatever he could
to postpone the Dreyfus trial in the hopes of averting renewed nationalist agitation while the Law of Separation he

had submitted to Parliament was under debate. By the time the Separation bill seemed assured of passage, the 1906 general election was only months away and the Civil Court of Appeals, one of the three sister courts of the United Court of Appeals, was so occupied with hearing voter registration suits that it could not sit with the other two appellate courts on the Dreyfus matter.

At long last, however, the election over, the full bench of the United Court of Appeals assembled on June 18, 1906, in the Palace of Justice to hear the case of Alfred Dreyfus, accused and twice convicted of the crime of treason. Twice before, the Palace had been the scene of climactic battles in the Dreyfus Affair — Zola's trial in 1898 and, a year later, the United Court's hearing on the question of revision. On the first occasion, the people of Paris had flocked to the Palace to fill every seat in its courtroom, to crowd its corridors and to congregate in a sullen, restless mob outside. Then Dreyfus's name had been hurled against the ancient walls in anger and contempt; then only a handful of brave men — Zola, Clemenceau, Scheurer-Kestner, Trarieux, Grimaux, Picquart — had dared to defend Dreyfus and, with him, the Republic. The following year the judicial proceedings of the United Court had been conducted in a more sedate atmosphere but then, too, suspense, tension and fear had hung heavy over a packed courtroom as Dreyfusard hopes warred with Army and nationalist determination to make Dreyfus's conviction stick. How different the scene was now as Alfred Dreyfus himself entered the Palace of Justice for the first time! The courtroom in which his case was to be tried was only half filled; aside from members of Dreyfus's family and a few of his friends, only a small knot of journalists and several lawyers anxious to witness the climax of a complicated legal tangle

were present. That the United Court would rule in favor of
Dreyfus was a foregone conclusion and the case, drained of
its suspense, no longer held any lure for the general public.
There was, however, one question that remained unanswered: would the United Court take upon itself the responsibility for Dreyfus's formal vindication or would it again
send his appeal to a military court-martial?

By this time the faith of Frenchmen in their Army's leaders
had fallen to such a low point that, with the exception of
Picquart, no one connected with the case, not even Dreyfus
himself, wanted to see it go before another military jury;
there was no reason to believe that a third court-martial
would return a different verdict than had the first or the
second. Picquart announced that he thought the case should
be carried to "its logical conclusions regardless of consequences," but it was widely recognized that his views were
influenced more by his bitterness toward Dreyfus than by a
realistic appraisal of the situation and little attention was
paid to him. Dreyfus, his faith in his superiors shattered at
last, was more than willing to accept a formal vindication
from a civil court. But, it was asked on every side, how could
the United Court avoid putting Dreyfus back in the hands of
military justice? French law required that in the case of a
military crime, a civil court of appeals had to remand to a
military court unless it could show that the crime in question
had not actually been committed. In other words, it would
not suffice for the United Court to establish that Dreyfus had
not written the bordereau; to clear him, the court would
have to show that the writing of the bordereau and the sending of it to the German military attaché had not been, in
fact, a crime!

Incredibly, the United Court succeeded in doing just that.

Persistent, careful questioning of military witnesses evoked the requisite admissions and concessions: the information referred to in the bordereau should never have been classified as either "secret" or "highly confidential"; much of it, it turned out, had been published in military journals before the time of the bordereau; the rest, according to the military experts' testimony, was so unimportant that its value to an unfriendly power could only be considered as negligible. On the strength of these findings, the United Court was able to show that the crime with which Dreyfus had been charged, the communication to enemy agents of the information listed in the bordereau, was not a crime and, on July 12, 1906, the court broke and annulled the judgment rendered at Rennes in 1899 and declared Dreyfus innocent of treason.

Dreyfus acquitted and his case closed at last! But in what a backhand way! He was innocent, not because another was guilty of the crime for which he had been twice convicted, but because, squirming through a legal loophole, France's highest court had managed to show that the crime itself had not been committed. For almost a decade people in every corner of the world had waited to hear the trumpets of justice sounding in France; now they heard the news of Dreyfus's acquittal accompanied only by the dull thud of legal compromise.

Since the amnesty law precluded punishment of the Affair's villains, all that remained was the matter of making reparations to its innocent victims. Adequate compensation for Dreyfus, or even for Picquart, was patently impossible and many who had been unjustly damned for the parts they had played in the Affair were already dead, but there were formal steps that could be taken to indicate the nation's remorse for past injustices and the Senate quickly voted to take them. Dreyfus and Picquart were officially reinstated in the Army — Dreyfus as a major and Picquart as a brigadier general; and, after paying pious and elaborate tributes to the patriotism of two of their former associates, whom only a few years earlier they had cast callously aside, the Senators voted to place busts of the men — Scheurer-Kestner and Trarieux, both now dead — in the lobby of the Senate.

Ten days after the United Court had declared him innocent, Major Alfred Dreyfus took part in a brief military ceremony in a small courtyard of the Ecole Militaire. Only a few paces from the spot where, twelve years earlier, he had been degraded under the eyes of a hostile mob, Dreyfus had his stripes restored to him and, as members of his family and a few friends watched, the cross of the Legion of Honor was pinned to his tunic. Drums rolled and bugles blew. Dreyfus, assailed by heartrending memories, struggled to maintain his composure. Another bugle blast and then the troops passed in review before Dreyfus, the sabers of their officers lifted in salute to him. The ceremony over, Dreyfus's son, Pierre, ran up to him and then, as he knelt to embrace the boy, Dreyfus finally wept. All at once he was surrounded by friends and relatives. A cry rang out — "Long Live Dreyfus!" "No," Dreyfus protested, humble in his happiness, "Long live the Republic! Long live the truth!" He looked around for Picquart and, finding him, thanked him for all he had done. The two men, at daggers points for so long, shook hands warmly.

During the ceremony, an enormous crowd had gathered outside the courtyard and as Dreyfus's carriage rolled out into the street, a great roar went up — "Long live Dreyfus!" "Long live Justice!" His arm around his son, Dreyfus smiled and waved to the people of France.

Epilogue

A YEAR after his rehabilitation Dreyfus resigned from the Army. He lived quietly with his family until the beginning of the 1914 World War when he rejoined the service and took command of an ammunition column. He led his men creditably through two of the most terrible battles of the war and in 1918 he was promoted to the rank of lieutenant colonel. He died in 1935 after a long illness.

Clemenceau became Premier of France in 1906 and in 1908 he made General Picquart his Minister of War. Although much was expected of Picquart in the way of army reforms, his conduct of his ministry was undistinguished. By a twist of fate his faulty horsemanship led to his death. It had been a fall from his horse that had convinced him in 1897 that he must put his suspicions of Esterhazy into writing lest he die without revealing what he knew; in January of 1914 he suffered another fall from a horse and though it was thought at first that his injuries were not serious, he died a few days later.

General Mercier fared better than he deserved. He had been elected to the Senate in 1900 by the ultra-conservative department of Loire-Inférieure and he kept his seat there until 1919. He died the next year at the age of eighty-eight. Du Paty re-enlisted in the Army as a rifleman second class in 1912 and at the beginning of the war was given command of an infantry regiment. He was wounded in battle and in 1916 he died of his wounds.

Immediately after Dreyfus's vindication, Edouard Drumont's fortunes went into a steep decline. Clerical anti-Semitism had died out completely and overt social anti-Semitism had become unfashionable. The circulation of *La Libre Parole* plummeted. Drumont tried to sell his paper and failed. He died in 1917 in poverty. Esterhazy never returned to France. For a time he supported himself in England by posing as an Irishman named Fitzgerald and selling articles highly critical of the country that had given him asylum to *L'Eclair*. In 1906 he assumed the name of Comte Jean-Marie de Voilemont and went to live in the small English village of Harpenden where he died in 1923 at the age of eighty-two.

Of all the leading figures in the Affair, only Clemenceau was still to play a major role in the history of France. Becoming Premier for the second time in 1917, he inspired his countrymen to resist the terrible onslaught of the German Army and rallied the Allied cause so successfully that he became known all over the world as "The Tiger of France." In 1918 it was Clemenceau who announced to the Chamber of Deputies that the provinces of Alsace and Lorraine were once again parts of France.

What can be made of the story in which these men played starring roles? Was the Dreyfus Affair really the high drama that it often seemed? Or was the absurdity of the United Court's "no crime" ruling a fitting finale to what was, after all, no more than a low comedy of human frailty and errors? The answers lie in the judgment history has made. The exact circumstances of Dreyfus's two convictions and eventual vindication have been largely forgotten. The world remembers that the case of an obscure army captain, unjustly accused of treason, confronted France with fateful choices; and that the French people, buffeted by a storm of antagonistic passions unleashed by the case, found at last that they could not rest easy until the "single injustice" of Dreyfus's conviction was righted.

The Dreyfus Affair brought France to grips with unresolved conflicts that had plagued her for more than a hundred years. Democratic or authoritarian government — which was best for France? The rights of the individual or those of society — which were to be paramount? Church or State — to which did the French citizen owe his political allegiance? Forced by the Affair to choose, Frenchmen opted finally for democracy and the supremacy of the individual and consented to a definitive separation of Church and State. During the years between Dreyfus's arrest and vindication France came through a trial of fire to commit herself finally to principles of her Revolution that she had previously embraced only in theory. Vindicating Alfred Dreyfus, France proclaimed to the world that she was, after all, jealous of her fame as a nation of "just judges and humane philosophers"; clearing Dreyfus's name, France cleared her own.

Because all revolutions against autocracy are beset by recurrent waves of counterrevolution, many scenes reminiscent of the drama played out in France at the turn of the century have been enacted since then in other countries where men strive to live by the rule of law. During the past two decades, the American people, especially, have found that excerpts of the Dreyfus story translate well.

In the 1950's, divisive fear and crippling self-mistrust blanketed the United States when Senator Joseph McCarthy, aided by irresponsible elements of the national press, persuaded millions of Americans to believe in the myth of an

American government riddled by agents of an enemy power. In the 1960's native apostles of an outmoded past rose to claim that the right of some white Americans to maintain the way of life they prefer takes precedence over the basic citizenship rights of their Negro countrymen. American Zolas and Clemenceaus warn that America's own Revolution is not yet fully won and the nation prepares for the struggle ahead. As the houselights dim, a new world audience settles back to watch.

The curtain rises again and again. History's plays are never quite over.

A NOTE ON SOURCES

ALTHOUGH the story of the Dreyfus Affair reads like a fanciful spy-thriller tale, an abundance of documentary evidence — court transcripts, official documents, newspaper and magazine articles, letters and memoirs — attests that its improbable people were real and that its incredible events happened. Two of the historians who have sifted through this wealth of material published careful studies of the Affair in 1955. These, *The Dreyfus Case: A Reassessment* by Guy Chapman (New York: Reynal and Company) and *Captain Dreyfus: The Story of a Mass Hysteria* by Nicholas Halasz (New York: Simon and Schuster), were relied on heavily in the preparation of this book. Older treatments, *The Dreyfus Affair* by Jacques Kayser (New York: Covici, Friede, 1931) and *The Dreyfus Case* by Fred C. Conybeare (London: George Allen, 1899), were also used.

Because the roles played in the Affair by anti-Semitism and by the unsettled relations between French Church and State are still in dispute, many sources for these subjects were consulted in the hope of gleaning from them as objective a point of view as possible. The following books and articles were the most helpful: on anti-Semitism, *The Foot of Pride* by Malcolm Hay (Boston: Beacon Press, 1950), *Anti-Semitism in Modern France*, Volume I, by Robert F. Byrnes (New Brunswick: Rutgers University Press, 1950), *Origins of Totalitarianism* by Hannah Arendt (New York: Harcourt, Brace, 1951), *The Jewish Problem in the Modern World* by James Parkes (New York and London: Oxford University Press, 1946) and *A Social and Religious History of the Jews*, Volume II, by Salo Wittmayer Baron (New York: Columbia University Press, 1937); on French Church and State, *The Catholic Church in the Modern World* by E. E. Y. Hales (Garden City, New York: Hanover House, 1958), *Church and State in France 1300–1907* by Arthur Galton

(London: Edward Arnold, 1907), "History of France" and "History of the Jews" in *The Catholic Encyclopedia* (New York: Robert Appleton, 1910) and "Dreyfus and After" by Joseph N. Moody in *The Bridge — A Yearbook of Judaeo-Christian Studies*, Volume II, edited by John M. Oesterreicher (New York: Pantheon Books, 1956).

From Dreyfus to Pétain by Wilhelm Herzog (New York: Creative Age Press, 1947), and two books by D. W. Brogan, *French Personalities and Problems* (New York: Knopf, 1947) and *The French Nation from Napoleon to Pétain* (New York: Harper, 1957), were used as sources for the history of modern France and information about Zola's and Clemenceau's careers and insights into their personalities were gained from *Zola* by Marc Bernard (New York: Grove Press, 1960), *Zola and His Time* by Matthew Josephson (New York: Macauley, 1928) and *Clemenceau and the Third Republic* by J. Hampden Jackson (The Macmillan Company, New York, 1948).

Details about the sufferings Dreyfus endured, his reactions and those of his family to the unfolding of his case, and letters he wrote and received, were found in *The Dreyfus Case* by Alfred and Pierre Dreyfus, translated and edited by Donald S. McKay (New Haven: Yale University Press, 1937), *Five Years of My Life* by Alfred Dreyfus (McClure, Phillips and Company, 1901) and *Lettres D'un Innocent: The Letters of Captain Dreyfus to His Wife* translated by L. G. Moreau (New York and London: Harper, 1899). *A Treasury of Great Reporting*, edited by Louis L. Snyder and Richard B. Morris (New York: Simon and Schuster, 1949), provided a French newspaper reporter's eyewitness account of Dreyfus's degradation, and a contemporary American's analysis of the forces at play in the Affair was found in *The Thought and Character of William James*, Volume II, by Ralph Barton Perry (Boston: Little, Brown, 1935). *The Tragedy of Dreyfus* by the English journalist G. W. Steevens (London and New York: Harper, 1899) was invaluable as a record of a perceptive observer's impressions of Dreyfus's trial at Rennes. *An Intimate Journal of the Dreyfus Case* by Maurice

Paléologue, an official of the French Foreign Office during the period of the Affair (New York: Criterion Books, 1957), was helpful as a measure of the impact the Affair had on Paris society.

Most illuminating on the place the Affair occupies in the history of western civilization were two books by Hans Kohn: *The Making of the Modern French Mind* (Princeton, New Jersey: D. Van Nostrand, 1955) and *The Modern World: 1848 to the Present* (New York: The Macmillan Company, 1963).

INDEX